P9-EMR-192

FASHION ME
A PEOPLE

FASHION ME A PEOPLE

Curriculum in the Church

MARIA HARRIS

Westminster/John Knox Press
Louisville, Kentucky

© 1989 Maria Harris

All rights reserved—no part of this book may be reproduced in any form without permission in writing from the publisher, except by a reviewer who wishes to quote brief passages in connection with a review in magazine or newspaper.

Scripture quotations from the Revised Standard Version of the Bible are copyrighted 1946, 1952, © 1971, 1973 by the Division of Christian Education of the National Council of the Churches of Christ in the U.S.A. and are used by permission.

Book design by Gene Harris

First edition

Published by Westminster/John Knox Press
Louisville, Kentucky

PRINTED IN THE UNITED STATES OF AMERICA

9 8

Library of Congress Cataloging-in-Publication Data

Harris, Maria.
   Fashion me a people.

   Includes index.
   1. Theology, Practical.   2. Christian education.
I. Title.
BV3.H34   1989   268   88-26117
ISBN 0-664-24052-6 (pbk.)

Contents

Foreword

This is the book on curriculum and the church I have been hoping someone would write. We have needed a book that helps pastors and other educators in the church understand curriculum in its large and important senses, connects it intimately with all that goes on in the church's life, and, at the same time, provides the kind of concrete stimulus to thought and action that enables readers to see how actual changes can be made in the way things are done. Well, here it is!

Perhaps this does not excite you as much as it does me. I can understand that. "Curriculum" is, unfortunately, a debased word. Its mention generates little interest or energy in most people. Some folks, because of their jobs or a task they've volunteered for, *have* to deal with curriculum—but most would rather not. Try picturing Maria Harris (at a dinner party, say) when she was writing this book:

"Maria, how are you? It's so nice to see you! Where've you been? What have you been up to?"

"I've been hiding away—writing a book, actually."

"How exciting! What's it on?"

"Curriculum. Curriculum and the church."

"Really. Well. How interesting. Yes."

The very word "curriculum" conjures up images of boxes piled on top of each other in out-of-the-way places,

packed with dull workbooks for children to fill out end-
lessly in Sunday school. Why would anyone want to write
a book on such a topic? How could such a topic *deserve* a
book?

The questions are irrelevant, because the image of curriculum lurking behind them is totally off the mark. It's
true that people have written books (and will probably
continue to write them) on how to survey, select, order,
and distribute the "right" boxes of workbooks for your
church. But this is not what curriculum is about at all.

Curriculum is about the mobilizing of creative, educative powers in such a way as to "fashion a people." Maria
Harris uses this wonderful image not only in the title of her
book but throughout, in order that we may see afresh how
deep and broad, how intricate and complex, and, finally,
how interesting and beautiful is the work of forming and
re-forming the "course" of the church's life. Curriculum is
not, in any of its most important senses, reducible to resource materials, no matter how good and how useful.
Rather, curriculum is an activity, a *practice* of a people.

Perhaps the news that curriculum is a practice rather
than an object does not pique your interest either. The
word "practice" has suffered hard times as well. We think
of sitting at the piano playing scales over and over again
—it seems routine, habitual, uncreative. Educators are ac-
cused of this all the time: "Practice is nothing but methods
and techniques." The implication is that practice is merely
following instructions, doing things that take little skill or
finesse, much less personal character, sensitivity, and
imagination. I suppose the fancy word "praxis" seeped
into our vocabularies to give doing things a little more
class, to indicate that thinking goes on sometimes too.

But "practice" is a good word, one that points to something that is essential and marvelous in human life and yet
difficult to achieve. The philosopher Alasdair MacIntyre
has defined a practice as "any coherent and complex form
of socially established cooperative human activity through
which goods internal to that form of activity are realized

in the course of trying to achieve those standards of excellence which are appropriate to, and partially definitive of, that form of activity, with the result that human powers to achieve excellence, and human conceptions of the ends and goods involved, are systematically extended" (*After Virtue*, p. 175; Notre Dame, Ind.: University of Notre Dame Press, 1981). This is a difficult sentence to read, because so much is packed into it. But it's worth reading several times, for it says several important things.

First, a practice is something "socially established"; it's been there awhile. Others have done it before us and have sustained it over time, because it has a value the community recognizes. Second, a practice is "cooperative human activity." It is something we do together, and we need each other in order to do it at all. Third, there are "goods internal to that form of activity." (By "goods," MacIntyre means moral goods, even spiritual goods, rather than, say, consumer goods.) And they come with doing the practice itself; they are not just commodities or results that the practice produces. Elements of really good human life are experienced and realized in the very activity of carrying out particular practices. Fourth, there are "standards of excellence" involved. This cooperative human activity can be done well or badly. If we do it well, something intrinsically good in human life can be experienced and even expanded. If we do it poorly, however, that good is lost to us. Excellent practice and poor practice are distinctly and discernibly different, and the achievement of the former requires skill, intelligence, knowledge, creativity, imagination, dedication, and discipline. Furthermore, such excellence must be taught, passed on from generation to generation—by those who carry out the practice with excellence themselves and value it enough to want to make sure others can come to do it as well. And finally, by learning a practice ourselves, and by learning more and more to do it well, our own lives are enhanced. Learning and carrying out some valuable practice provides, in itself, an important form of moral and spiritual education. Our

powers are increased and our minds and spirits are en-
larged.

Not every activity is a practice in this sense. Painting is;
shaving is not. MacIntyre says baseball is a practice, while
tic-tac-toe is not. (Commenting on this, Jeffrey Stout points
out that, in baseball, the goods internal to the practice are
"what Mattingly achieves, Red Smith appreciated, and
Steinbrenner violates" [*Ethics After Babel*, p. 303; Boston:
Beacon Press, 1988].) In any case, the crucial point for us
is that curriculum is a practice while providing resource
materials is not—*except* insofar as the activity of providing
resource materials has become an intrinsic part of the
larger practice of curriculum.

Fashion Me a People is the second in a trio of books
being published by Westminster / John Knox Press concerning various dimensions of the church's comprehensive practice of Christian education. (The other two are
Daniel O. Aleshire's *Faithcare: Ministering to All God's
People Through the Ages of Life* [1988] and *Gathered for
Learning* [forthcoming] by Freda Gardner and Craig
Dykstra.) Maria Harris shows in this book how curriculum
is the *practice* of fashioning a people, in response to and
in cooperation with the fashioning of people that God is
carrying out. Harris describes this practice in such a way
that its meaning and internal "goods" become apparent to
us. She shows us how this practice has been sustained and
carried on by the church throughout its existence. She
insists that this practice be fundamentally shared, corporate, cooperative human activity; either that, or it is not
the practice of curriculum at all. Above all, Harris invites
us into this practice ourselves and teaches it to us. The
excellences involved in this practice are made evident.
And it becomes clear to us from her description of them
that, as we become more accomplished in this practice, we
ourselves will grow and mature.

Obviously, this is not a simple "how-to" book on church
curriculum. But it is a very practical book. By reading it
with care, and especially by reading it with one another,

members and leaders of congregations can discover in it the very concrete resources they need to form, carry on, and re-form the course of their Christian life together through the day-to-day efforts of their educational ministry.

Princeton Theological Seminary   CRAIG DYKSTRA

Acknowledgments

I have been thinking of curriculum issues ever since I was a graduate student at Teachers College, Columbia University, where Dwayne Huebner's classes on curriculum inevitably provoked serious thought. At the same time, I was also working with Mary Tully at Union Theological Seminary, studying and practicing the ways in which artistic attitudes and approaches could transform everything. The two interests, art and curriculum, come together in this book, but without the initial influence of those two great teachers, that would never have happened for me.

More recently, I have become persuaded of the critical importance of distinguishing between the curriculum of education and the curriculum of schooling, an insight of Gabriel Moran's that lies at the core of this book. I attempt to develop this insight in my working out the forms of church life as a whole curriculum, believing that Moran's insight is crucial for further curriculum design. Most recently, my conversation and collaboration with Craig Dykstra, who generously and graciously made suggestions to improve this text, have educated me toward a clearer, more concise rendering of the proposals I make here, and of curriculum in the church.

To those four people, my appreciation and gratitude. What is of value here is theirs; what is lacking is mine.

13

Introduction

We find the image of God as a potter fashioning a people in both the Hebrew Bible and the New Testament. The prophet Isaiah reminds us that we do not make ourselves and points out the foolishness in thinking that we do. "Shall the potter be regarded as the clay; that the thing made should say of its maker, 'He did not make me'; or the thing formed say of him who formed it, 'He has no understanding'?" (Isa. 29:16). Jeremiah also focuses on this image in an even more familiar text: "Behold, like the clay in the potter's hand, so are you in my hand, O house of Israel" (Jer. 18:6b). In Romans, Paul uses the image too, sobering us with a reference to "vessels of wrath" at the same time that he graces us with the imagery of a God making known the riches of divine glory for the "vessels of mercy" we might hope to become (Rom. 9:20–24).

This imagery of a Creator Spirit who is a Divine Artist at work in the cosmos can be interpreted in two ways.[1] The first interpretation envisions a God who is essentially separate from what has been made and remains outside it. The second interpretation, familiar to poets and mystics, assumes instead that God is a brooding, hovering, indwelling Presence, always acting from within creation: renewing it, cherishing it, loving it. When the creation being fashioned is a people, they must not think of themselves as separated from the source of life. Rather, they live and breathe and have their being through and with and in the Divinity. The mystic Julian of Norwich said it simply: We are enclosed in God, and God is enclosed in us.[2]

In this book we examine the creating of curriculum as artistic educational work contributing to this fashioning of a people. As we do that, it is the second interpretation of creating that guides us. I propose that we begin with the assumption that curricular work is holy work, religious work, and that God dwells with us as we do it, in the midst of each of the human processes we choose. God stays within us as the source of the creative power that moves us both to will and to accomplish. We are held in the divine hands, and the grace of God and the Spirit of God abide within us, enabling us to become what we are called to be.

At the same time, however, because we are made in the image of the Creator God, we too are fashioners. Our human vocation is to be in partnership with God to fashion even as we are being fashioned, attempting to realize our artistic capacities as this happens. For to the question, "Who is fashioning?" the response is, "God and ourselves." And the medium we are asked to concentrate on here as the "stuff" or material of our work is the set of forms "traditioned" to us through the centuries by the Christian church, the set of forms that, taken together, comprise the curriculum of the church.

The Forms of Church Curriculum

The first time these forms are named for us is in the book of Acts. There we find in one place the most detailed description of the first Christian community doing what will in time become the classical activities of ecclesial ministry: kerygma, proclaiming the word of Jesus' resurrection; didache, the activity of teaching; leiturgia, coming together to pray and to re-present Jesus in the breaking of bread; koinonia, or community; and diakonia, caring for those in need.

In Acts, the kerygma is first announced: "This Jesus God

raised up, and of that we all are witnesses" (Acts 2:32).
There too the following account is given:

> And they continued steadfastly in the teaching of the apos-
> tles and in the communion of the breaking of bread and in
> the prayers. . . . And all who believed were together and
> held all things in common and would sell their possessions
> and goods and distribute them among all according as any-
> one had need. And continuing daily with one accord in the
> temple, and breaking bread in their houses, they took their
> food with gladness and simplicity of heart, praising God and
> being in favor with all the people. (Acts 2:42, 44–47)

These few verses are the first portrait of church curriculum we have, although the word "curriculum" is of course
not used.[3] In the description, Luke gives us the central
elements, or the set of forms, that embody the course of
the church's life. In this book I propose to show that the
fashioning and refashioning of this set of forms is the core
of the educational ministry of the church. I also propose
to show that the forms themselves are the primary curriculum of the church, the course of the church's life, and
that in fashioning these forms we fashion the church. And
because *we* are the church, the fashioning of the forms
becomes the fashioning of us.

The entire course of the church's life—such a meaning
of curriculum has been emerging over the last several
decades. Designers and planners of curriculum, as well as
general educators in the church, have come to see the
need for a broader, more extensive, and more complete
basic understanding of curriculum than is often used.
Widespread agreement exists today that although the
meaning of curriculum from which the church works includes schooling and teaching—or didache—and involves
printed, published resources, curriculum is a far broader
reality. Necessarily, it includes the other forms through
which the church educates, such as worship, proclamation, community, and service. Today we are moving toward a refusal to limit curriculum as it has been limited in
the past. Curriculum is more than materials and tech-

nique; it is intended for adults as well as children; and it
is offered through more forms of education than what is
called schooling. We are moving toward a creative vision
that sees all the facets of the church's life as the church
curriculum, with curricular materials named simply
"resources."

The Plan of This Book

We will explore this fuller meaning, as well as examine
how to go about realizing it in practice. Part One, "The
Context," offers three points of departure in curriculum
fashioning and therefore in people fashioning. First, the
church is a people with a pastoral vocation (chapter 1).
Second, the church is a people with an educational vocation (chapter 2). Third, when we participate in the educational work of shaping the forms that comprise the
church's life, we are shaping its curriculum—and that curriculum is shaping us (chapter 3). Such an understanding
is admittedly broad, but I am convinced that only a meaning with this much breadth can guide us today.

Part Two, "The Vocation," is more specific, examining
each of the forms of education in the church mentioned
above. Chapter 4 concentrates on koinonia, the curriculum of community; chapter 5 focuses on leiturgia, the curriculum of prayer; chapter 6 on didache, the curriculum
of teaching; chapter 7 on kerygma, the curriculum of proclamation; and chapter 8 on diakonia, the curriculum of
reaching out in service. Part Three, "The Planning" (chapter 9), returns to the artistic vocation of fashioning in order
to explore ways people in congregations can plan their
work, putting the insights of the previous chapters into
practice.

For Whom Is the Book Intended?

Obviously, this book can benefit those who are instructors or teachers in the church and those who are curriculum planners—persons with titles such as Director of

Education, Minister of Education, Sunday School Super-
intendent, or Curriculum Designer. But if education in
the church is indeed the forming of the entire life of the
church, then the book also becomes important for those
involved in each church ministry, whether that is prayer,
community, service, or outreach, and whether those persons are clergy or laity. Indeed, because we are a people,
we are called to come together across the boundaries of
preacher and teacher, clergy and laity, professional and
amateur, part-time and full-time, and realize that in partnership with one another and our Creator God we are
engaged in the same fashioning work begun in Genesis.
Unless we *do* come together, many features of church life
that educate, features by which and in which the Christian
vocation is learned, will not be spoken of, thought of as
educational, or mined for the riches they are.

Thus the book is offered as a serious yet understandable
theoretical base for design, as a set of procedures to follow,
and as a fresh vision of curriculum for the church. I hope
that, received in the same spirit, it may provide the lever-
age we need to move toward a more vital educational
understanding and practice and that it may be itself a
vessel through which a people can be fashioned, to the
honor and praise and glory of the brooding, caring Potter,
in whose hands we never cease to be held.

PART ONE

THE CONTEXT

1

Church: A People with a Pastoral Vocation

No image has so captured our Christian imaginations in recent years as has the image of ourselves as a people. Although various models of the church, such as herald, servant, institution, and congregation, continue to influence us,[1] the dominating self-understanding is increasingly the church as a people. Perhaps this one emerges as most compelling because it takes our humanness seriously. Being a people, a community of persons, means that all of us are flesh and blood, heirs to both the heights and the depths of everything that goes into being human. It takes the incarnation seriously and suggests that we have allowed into our spirits the truth that the Word has become flesh (John 1). And because we have accepted that, we have also allowed into our spirits the truth that the Word continues to become flesh, today, in us.

The Word continually becoming flesh, *in us*, completes the image. For not only are we coming to understand ourselves more and more as a people; we now realize that we are a people with a pastoral vocation. The truth of our baptism and confirmation is confronting us regularly, and we are beginning to see that being incorporated into this people carries responsibilities with it. No longer is it enough to be passive members, receiving a word told us by someone else, filing that word away to be taken out for a reading now and then. No longer is it enough to leave the work of the church to pastors and ordained leaders, as if the total responsibility was theirs. Instead, we are realizing that the word of God is addressing us, saying something to us, making demands on us, and asking us to live that word in our lives. We are a people called by the gospel, called to make a difference in our world.

The active attempt to make this difference is the heart of the pastoral vocation. The pastoral vocation, as the phrase suggests, is a call to, and a demand for, a particular way of living. The particularity can be summed up in the word "pastoral," which implies a caring for, and a relationship to, persons, and an active and practical engagement in the work of Christian ministry. We are called to care: for ourselves, for one another, for the earth which is our home. We are called to take seriously our relation to God and to all God's creatures, both within and beyond the church. We are called to end our isolation from others by living each day of our lives rooted in love, rooted in the Christ. And we are called to believe that in doing so, we fulfill our destiny as a people of God.

A recent church document sums up this vocation:

> For by its very nature the Christian vocation is also a vocation to the ministry. No part of the structure of a living body is merely passive but each has a share in the functions as well as in the life of the body. So, too, in the body of Christ, which is the Church, the whole body, "according to the functioning in due measure of each single part, derives its increase" (Eph. 4:16). Indeed, so intimately are the parts linked and interrelated in this body (cf. Eph. 4:16) that the members who fail to make their proper contribution to the development of the church must be said to be useful neither to the Church nor to themselves.[2]

We can understand this vocation more deeply when we realize that the church is a people with a mission. Mission means sending. The mission of the people who are the church is to go into the world and to be in the world as Jesus was, as the revelation of God. The mission of the people who are the church is to reveal God as present to the world, as a God who cares for the world and is in an ongoing relation to the world. The mission is to reveal a God who works through active and practical ministry in the world—a world so loved that, in the words of John 3:16, the only-begotten Son of this God was given as gift to the world.

What do the people do so that God is revealed through them? What they are sent to do is ministry. And ministry is serving.[3] We are "missioned" into the world as servants of God.

We are called to serve in a number of diverse though deeply connected ways. In the five chapters of Part Two we will look carefully at the classical, historic ways this service has been carried out: through koinonia (community), leiturgia (prayer and worship), didache (teaching), kerygma (proclamation), and diakonia (outreach). We will look even more specifically at how we educate persons to perform these ministries. For now, however, as we begin unfolding the pastoral vocation, we need to look at the roots of these specific ministries. These are the roots we discover in both Protestant and Catholic traditions, each of which honors the triple office of the Christ. These are the roots of ministry seen as priestly, prophetic, and political, each aspect continuing the work of Jesus, who was himself an embodiment of the vocation to be priest and prophet and king.

The Heidelberg Catechism puts this vocation distinctly in Questions 31 and 32.

> Question 31: Why is He called Christ, that is, anointed? Answer: Because He is ordained of God the Father, and anointed with the Holy Spirit, to be our chief Prophet and Teacher, who fully reveals to us the secret counsel and will of God concerning our redemption; and our High Priest, who by the one sacrifice of his body has redeemed us, and ever liveth to make intercession for us with the Father; and our eternal King, who governs us by his word and Spirit, and defends and preserves us in the redemption obtained for us. Question 32: But why art thou called a Christian? Answer: Because by faith I am a member of Christ and thus

a partaker of his anointing, in order that I also may confess his name (Prophet), may present myself a living sacrifice of thankfulness to Him (Priest), and may with free conscience fight against sin and the Devil in this life, and hereafter, in eternity, reign with him over all creatures (King).

The Catechism also takes care that the young may be initiated into these understandings. For in the Junior Heidelberg Catechism, Question 69 is the same as 31, above, and then Question 70 is put both more simply and more succinctly:

Question 70: To what end art thou a partaker of his anointing?
Answer: *That I also may be a prophet, a priest and a king.*

Similarly, the documents of Vatican II reiterate these vocations. To quote *Lumen Gentium,* the decree on the Church: "These faithful are by baptism made one body with Christ and are established among the People of God. They are in their own way made sharers in the priestly, prophetic, and kingly functions of the Christ."[4]

What both documents point to, therefore, is this central teaching, present from the beginnings of Christianity: the pastoral vocation has at least three components. As a priestly people, we are called to hallowing, blessing, and remembering, and to the works of teaching, prayer, and preserving traditions. As a prophetic people, we are called to speak the word of justice and to embody God's pathos —God's manifest and continuing grieving over human suffering and human sin. As a kingly people—or better (since the word "king" is a governing or administrative title, as well as gender exclusive), as a political people[5]— we are called first to shape and design our own polity, our ways of being together, so that these ways enable and enhance the proclamation of the gospel and the living of the gospel in our own Christian communities; and, second, we are called to bring the institutions and systems of our world into account so that they too are enabling and empowering for life on this planet. We are to claim our authority to do that.

To put all this another way, the pastoral vocation as priestly involves living fully in the present, assisted by the visions and memory of the past. As prophetic, this living fully in the present is assisted by the visions and hopes of the future. And as political, this vocation demands that we be an intelligent and conscious body politic, living fully in the present through systems and forms that are worthy of us as a people called in baptism. These three were, and are, embodied in Jesus. And because of this we can be forewarned that they ought not to be understood too easily or conventionally. Indeed, all false notions of priestly, prophetic, and political ministry are unmasked and changed in the life of this man from Nazareth. This implies, for those who follow him, that in us they are meant to be changed, transformed, and unmasked too.

The Tensions in the Vocation

As we begin to take seriously this call which we have received, we need to name and recognize the forces that have brought us to this new view of ourselves as a people with a pastoral vocation. Three tensions are especially evident. In choosing the word "tensions" I want to emphasize not so much its connotation as mental, emotional, or nervous strain as its evocation of a tautness and a stretching, that positive condition created when important forces pull against each other. Tension seen this way suggests an artistic idea and marks the presence of intelligence. Without the internal resistance that tension calls forth, we rush too quickly to completed activity, bypassing the chastening work of examined development and complex fulfillment. The lack of tension causes collapse. Tension is needed. Tension is good. And the tensions with us in the church today are at least three: the tensions between the personal and the communal, between the local and the global, and between the clergy and the laity. Let us consider each of these in turn.

The Personal and the Communal

Although the church has always championed the integrity of each of its members (at least in theory), the outcome of this support has often been more in the direction of individualism than of personalism. Elements in the Reformation—for example, in holding up the ideal of the individual before God—unwittingly contributed to a notion that often seemed to be in opposition to human community. Even today, in many Christian communions, it is not unusual to be taught that religion is what a man does with his solitariness.[6]

At the extreme, this ideal of the mature person often became someone capable not only of individualism but of "rugged" individualism; someone able to make decisions and judgments autonomously, alone; someone who could always be totally rational in all situations, even if being rational was inappropriate. We have only to look at some of the dominant models of adulthood in our society to see how ingrained this individualism has become, especially in the worlds of business, government, and the military. The loner as hero becomes the epitome of human success, and looking out for "number one" the quintessential human vocation.

This vision of human maturity is being shattered, however, by the force and power of personalism, which has come into its own in this century. In contrast to individualism, personalism emphasizes the understanding that all (not just each) human beings have equal dignity and that all (not just each) human beings have the right to the abundant gifts of the Creator. This set of beliefs draws special attention, just as the gospel does, to the marginal of the world, the great so-called underclass of the poor, the disenfranchised, and the ill. It draws particular attention to the poorest of the poor in every society, namely, women; to the unequal distribution of the world's goods; and to the disproportionate burdens placed on the backs of people of color. It knows, as Martin Luther King, Jr., taught, that it is a cruel jest to tell people to pull themselves up by their bootstraps when they have no boots. And it causes the realization that the doctrine of rugged individualism is in actuality a celebration of only some individuals—more often than not, powerful, wealthy, white men.

The greatest contribution of personalism, however, has been the exploration of what it means to be a human person and the discovery that to *be* as a person means *to be with*. That is to say that we are only fully persons when we are in community and in communion with one another. We are related to one another not only by baptism but by blood. We are responsible to one another for life and for death. Although we may not be our brothers' and sisters' keepers, we are our brothers' and sisters' brothers and sisters. In other words, being *persons* is possible only if we are in community; and our existence, humanly, as communities falls short whenever the personhood of even one in the community is denied.

Thus, the first tension influencing our pastoral vocations is the personal and the communal. Maintaining the tension, rather than collapsing it, is critical. I need to emphasize this because often in the church we find ourselves taking sides and choosing investment in either one or the other, but not both. In our rush to celebrate each person, we feel we must downplay persons-in-relation, or relations with the nonhuman world: animals, plant life, earth. Or, in contrast, when we realize that no one can be whole, or blessed, or happy until all are whole, blessed, and happy, we stress community and begin to downplay the genuine needs, hopes, and dreams of each person in this community.

When we come to consider the curricula of leiturgia and kerygma in chapters 5 and 7 we shall see what this involves educationally. For now, however, it is instructive to note that the personal and communal tension is often evident in the related ministries of prayer/worship and acting for justice. In teaching spirituality or prayer or piety, for example, we may be so intent on quiet time where we go apart and rest awhile, or on the relation between Jesus and *me,* that we forget to return to the place where we are called to be together, especially the Table. In teaching justice or prophecy or social action, as a contrasting example, we may be so intent on caring for those in desperate need of justice that we step on or step over the desperate needs of those being asked to *do* justice.

The point to make here is that both are necessary. The pastoral vocation is alert and alive when it holds on to both poles at the same time. But maintaining this tension is possible only when the vocation itself is seen as personal *and* communal. It is a vocation that belongs to no person if it belongs only to one. That is why it is situated in the midst of the *ekklēsia,* the *basileia,* the church itself.

assembly, gathering, commonwealth

The Local and the Global

This brings us to a second tension that is shaping our pastoral vocation in today's church: the tension between the church understood and experienced as local and the church understood and experienced as universal, worldwide, global. The planet itself has taken on the characteristics of a global village and the church has become self-conscious of itself in a similar way. Undoubtedly influenced by television and instant communication worldwide, we have begun to see that when Columbus, Ohio, moves, Rio de Janeiro quivers; when Iran speaks, Anchorage, Alaska, listens; and when San Francisco hurts, Amsterdam feels compelled toward healing.

In some ways, this situation is novel, but it is not really a new tension in the church. In *New Ministries: The Global Context,* William Burrows reminds us that

> there is a Johannine vision of the church, common especially in Asia, which tended to see each local church gathered around the mystically present Christ—its center of unity—as *the* church. [Another] vision, however, came to dominate in the West. In it there is an emphasis on a global unity of everyone and everything in Christ, a unity represented by the ministers who exercise authority in his name.[7]

What has often happened historically, again, is that church people have chosen one vision over the other. Either we are an autonomous, local congregation, ultimately answerable only to ourselves before God, or we are a universal organism, with each local unit a cell necessarily related to all the other cells worldwide.

Today such a choice is less and less tenable. We have reached the time when we must hold on to both visions. Maintaining the tensions, we need to take responsibility for what we do and are locally, but always in the context of a church where all are members one of the other. Neither vision can be allowed to dominate, for if one should, we would be in danger of isolation and self-centeredness and self-preoccupation, on the one hand, or of narrow, uninformed authoritarianism from a distance on the other. This means we may champion the idea of small house churches and basic Christian communities alert to their own contexts and circumstances but only in the context of an understanding that each local community will forge its identity in terms of its global relations within the entire church.

Maintaining this second tension is particularly incumbent on churches in the United States for several reasons. One reason is that, since we are a community of churches situated in the country that uses and has access to most of the world's resources, the pastoral vocation compels us to work toward the reordering of their distribution. This in turn involves embracing a theology of relinquishment. Because we are churches set in the midst of global want, the need of others (both within and beyond our own boundaries) is our need too.

Another reason is that, since we are a church whose population rate continues either to stabilize or to fall, our position in the world church must move toward increasing openness to being influenced by other peoples. If present demographic patterns continue, the church of the year 2000 will see 58 percent of all Christians, and 70 percent of all Catholic Christians, living south of the equator.[8] What this implies for our sense of ourself as a people is dramatic. Those with whom we are coming into partnership are people of antiquity, reminding us that history began neither in Europe nor in North America but in Asia and Africa. Thus the theology of our local churches cannot be a theology only of Europe and North America. Also, they are people of youth. The median age of this world church is growing increasingly younger, even as the U.S. church grows older. Therefore the attitudes of our local churches cannot be those of only one age group. Finally, our new partners are dynamic people, in the springtime of their new, modern life, remarkable for their initiative, optimism, and freshness in the world church. For local churches in the U.S. church, this can only mean our need to reassess our ways of coming together and being together where they are moribund and in need of originality and imagination.

A further implication of maintaining the tension between the local and the global has barely touched us. This is our need to be in conversation and dialogue with religions besides our own. As the church becomes increasingly more conscious of the context in which it exists, we will be impelled more and more toward local Jewish-Christian, Muslim-Christian, and Buddhist-Christian dialogue and relations. Indeed, it is likely that we will find ourselves increasingly shocked that for decades we have existed on the same block or in the same town with peoples of other faiths and, it is hoped, appalled that we have made virtually no move toward community. As we begin such conversations, we will also discover newer, richer, and more complete understandings of the God who is the God of us all, locally and universally, the God before whom we dwell under the same stars, the same moon, and the same sun.

The Clergy and the Laity

A third tension provoking us toward a new and renewed pastoral vocation is the changed situation growing in the midst of the church between clergy and laity. To some degree, conflict as well as cooperation has always accompanied this relation. But in our time, sometimes imperceptibly and sometimes loudly and publicly, we are beginning to realize that the clergy-laity form of being the church is undergoing drastic revision.[9] The actual tension here is not really embodied in people. Rather, it is found in the increasingly inappropriate division of ourselves into clergy and laity. This is especially marked in reference to the language we use of ourselves, which is in turn shaped by symbolism, setting, and power.

With reference to language, the distinction etched in stone between some of us as clergy and some of us as lay persons has fallen on hard times. An examination of the adjective "lay" gives some clues why this is so. Two major dictionaries begin defining "lay" by stating what it is *not* rather than what it *is:* lay means "not in clerical orders"; "not in holy orders: not of the clergy: not clerical: not ecclesiastical [!]" They continue, "not of or from a particular profession: not having special training or knowledge: unprofessional: common, ordinary." A third dictionary, besides agreeing with these, adds "inexperienced, ignorant and uncultivated" and concludes with the information that in cards a "lay" hand is one with few or no trumps.[10]

Language is shaped and reshaped by what it intends to symbolize. The language of "clergy" and "laity" is less and less appropriate today, precisely because it does not attend to the symbolic reality it attempts to convey. The ordained and the nonordained are not related as haves and have-nots, as sacred and secular, as illuminati (enlightened ones) and ignorant. Instead, our differing roles are complementary to one another and often overlapping. As never before, except perhaps in New Testament times, the far more apparent symbolism is (once again) of a people, where some are "apostles, some prophets, some evangelists, some pastors and teachers," but all are together for the building up of the body of the Christ (Eph. 4:11–13).

What does distinguish (but still does not separate) us are the settings and the places where we live out our voca-

tions. Although bivocational ministries among the ordained are beginning to be exercised once again (remember Paul the tentmaker, Peter the fisherman), it remains
true that the pastoral vocation is lived out by some of us
as full-time, as official spokespersons for the church. Without downplaying those in the church who are also full-
time, such as directors of religious education, directors of
Christian education, organists, and sextons, it remains true
that there is usually at least one person in every ecclesial
community whose ministry is, in Gabriel Fackre's felici-
tous term, a ministry of "identity."[11] This is the ministry
whose specific purpose is to keep reminding the people of
the Source of their lives and their raison d'être. In such
persons is embodied not only the pastoral vocation but the
pastoral office. They are the ones chosen by the community to speak for it, to represent it, and to be its officers.

The far more common setting for the pastoral vocation,
however, is the workplace outside the gathered church—
whether that workplace is the home, the office, the hospital, the farm, the factory, or the publishing company. The
vast majority of us exercise our priestly, prophetic, and
political vocations in everyday settings: on buses, in stores,
at lunch counters, in our kitchens. The mutuality between
clergy and laity that arises from these different settings
reminds those in the pastoral office of their involvement
in the common humanity of us all.[12] It reminds them that
they are *a part of* rather than *apart from.* At the same
time, their exercise of the priestly, prophetic, and political
vocation is more usually the work of reminding those
caught up in the business—and busyness—of life that their
lives must have times for the "one thing necessary." Put
in more poetic language, ordained and nonordained know
they must minister *in* and *of* and *on account of* one another. And they must love one another.

Most of all, however, they must share power. They
must share the power to do and to act as well as the
power to receive and to wait. No longer is the pastoral
office the only locus of power. Instead, by reason of bap-

tism and confirmation all have been given the power that resides in the grace of the Christ: the power to heal, to remember, to bless; the power to do justice and love mercy and walk humbly with God. In all of us resides the power to be poor in spirit, to be merciful, and to mourn. In all of us resides the power of vocation, of mission, and of ministry.[13] If this is true, if these powers do reside in all of us, then a deeper and more extensive understanding of how the church is to educate this people than we have usually had is required. To the nature of such education, we turn in chapter 2.

REFLECTION AND PRACTICE

Exercise 1: Questions for Musing and for Discussion

1. Reflect on your religious autobiography. Recall and name three events or situations when you became aware of your pastoral vocation.

2. Are there persons in your life whom you associate with moving you into this vocation? If so, who are (were) they and what did they do?

3. What are some ways you believe you—and your church, locally and worldwide—are called to live out the universal priestly vocation of ministry (the ministries of healing, blessing, teaching, and remembering)?

4. What are some ways you believe you—and your church, locally and worldwide—are called to live out the prophetic vocation (the ministries of justice and concern for others)?

5. What are some ways you believe you—and your church, locally and worldwide—are called to live out the political vocation (the shaping and reshaping of the forms

of church and public life), so that it is a place where all are welcome?

Exercise 2: A Ritual for Ordaining to the Pastoral Vocation*

Your local congregation or parish has decided to take seriously the vocation of all of its members to the pastoral vocation. In this exercise, you are invited to plan a service of ordination that alerts the congregation to this vocation and celebrates it. The exercise may be for an actual ordination; or it may be a "How would we go about doing this if it should happen?" exercise. Include in your plan answers to these questions:

- What are your objectives for this ritual?
- Who are to be included in this ritual?
- How long will the ritual be?
- Where will you choose to hold this ritual?
- What will be the form of the ritual and what actions will be included in it?
- What scripture texts will you use?
- Who in the community will do what?

*An alternative ritual could be one planned for someone whose pastoral vocation is being celebrated, e.g., a person working on a housing project, a lawyer devoting time *pro bono,* a new parent, or a student beginning high school or college.

Exercise 3: Discovering the History of Your Church

This exercise is one in which a group of persons (such as the Christian education committee, the justice committee, or the board of deacons) agree to interview the oldest members of the church to discover their memories of the history of the parish and then to report back. The particular foci of the interviews are to be changing models of the church over the decades, as well as the sense of the personal-communal, local-global, and clergy-laity tensions.

Exercise 4: How Do You Look at the World?

For this exercise, you are required to have two maps: Map 1 is the ordinary Mercator map, familiar from schooling; Map 2 is the world map in equal-area presentation (the Peters projection), available in many bookstores or through Church World Service, 475 Riverside Drive, New York, N.Y. 10115.

- Display the two maps next to each other.
- Take time to compare the two maps.
- Notice especially:
    The placement of the United States on each map
    The placement of the equator on each map
    The land mass of various countries and continents on each map
    The representation on each map of places where whites have traditionally lived
- Complete the exercise by drawing out and discussing the implications each of the projections has
    For our understanding of the world
    For mission in the world
    For ministry in the world
    For the priestly, the prophetic, and the political dimensions of the pastoral vocation

2

Church: A People with an Educational Vocation

In chapter 1 we explored the nature of the church as a people with a pastoral vocation. In this chapter we take up two further questions: (1) What meaning of education will serve us best in realizing that vocation? (2) When a revised meaning is proposed, what are the implications for the church as educator? The work of chapter 3, which deals specifically with curriculum, cannot be approached unless we have first confronted the difficult issue of what we mean, precisely, when we speak of *education* in the church.

Present Understandings

Education in the church is lifelong. This is too obvious to bear repetition, too obvious until we begin to see how major are the revisions this belief demands in our educational curriculum. Still, education in the church as lifelong must be our starting point because the pastoral vocation is lifelong. For a people called by the gospel in baptism and confirmation, there is no time in our life when that call ends. Our education into it is ongoing and ought to become increasingly richer and more complex as we develop through adulthood.

When we come to implementing this idea of lifelong education, however, we confront a twofold *mis*understanding which continues to exercise control over the educational imagination in this country, despite our convictions. The first misunderstanding is that education is for children. The popular press, the media, and books about education all convey, whether implicitly or explicitly, the basic conviction that education is a work devoted to children. The misunderstanding is so deep that when we try to speak of education that is not for children, we must give it a name such as "adult" education to distinguish it from the (so-called) real thing.

The second misunderstanding gripping the educational imagination is the false identification of education with only one of its forms: schooling. In this view, the participants in education are always "instructors" or "learners"; the place of education is necessarily a school (or a setting that replicates the school); the stuff of education is books and chalkboards and lesson plans; and the process involved is mental activity. The word "form" is especially important here. When you or I attempt to broaden the notion of education beyond the school, we are given as operating language the basic assumption that we are talking about *"in*formal" learning. Or, to put the matter in another and more direct way, school is the one educational setting with form. Anything else is without form, or at best, "informal" education—which too often translates loosely as "not really serious."

Complicating these misunderstandings is the truth that we are, of course, talking about children when we talk about education. To say, "It is not only about children" is not the same as, "Don't bother about children." Of course education should bother about children! But the truth of education is that if it is assumed to be only for children, it will not be good for anyone—especially not for children. Children will observe that they are the only ones being attended to and will long for the time when they are done being "educated." They will think of education as something that can be "finished." My own educational work is a search to find new ways of speaking about this, since the language we use to describe our work has enormous power, either to support or to undermine what we are attempting to do.

Equally important, education does include schooling— and books and lessons and instructors and learners. But again, as crucial and important as it is, schooling is still only one of the forms of education. In addition, "It is not only about schooling," often is interpreted as, "Don't bother about schooling." What is needed is a way of understanding, and of speaking about education, which, while taking children and schooling seriously, refuses to collapse the meaning of education into the work with children that is done in school.

This is especially critical for the church viewed as a people who have a lifelong, pastoral vocation. For we are a people of all ages, who learn in different settings and in diverse ways. Because of that, we require the use of many forms that can help us realize our vocation, and we require a meaning of education attentive to these. In order to help us see what the education of a people called to such a lifelong vocation involves, I propose a broad and extensive understanding of education as artistic work. Education, like all other artistic endeavors, is a work of giving form. More specifically, it is a work especially concerned with the creation, re-creation, fashioning, and refashioning of form.[1]

Education as Formgiving

One of the greatest educators I have ever known was Mary Tully, my mentor at Union Seminary in New York. She once gave us a simple exercise connected with clay. We played with the clay first and discovered something of what it could do—for example, it could be stretched only so long, then it would break; it became hardened by the air. Then she asked us to blindfold ourselves and gave us the following directions:

"A form exists within the clay you are holding in your hands, and you are to discover it. As you work with the clay, let it work with you. Give yourself time, concentrate, and you will encounter a form taking shape. You will be able to feel it, to sense it, to know it. When that happens, you can take off the blindfold and work from there."[2]

Through the years I have often done that same exercise with others and realized that Mary Tully was right. The form is there, waiting to be found, created, and re-created. The power of the clay image is that it teaches us the nature of forming, informing, formation, and formgiving in education. The work is ongoing, in mutuality with material, and open always to further meaning. The molding of clay is a concrete metaphor illuminating the work of education as the fashioning and refashioning of the forms that human life offers, the forms we shape as artists at the same time we allow those forms to shape us. For as human beings we are always extending our hands into life and into experience in order to give them form.

The work of education is giving flesh to, and embodying, form. But form is not an arbitrary organizational element —one among many. Rather, as every artist knows, form is the actual shape of content. Form is a marshaling of materials in relation to one another. It is a setting of boundaries and limits. It is a discipline, an ordering and a fashioning according to need.[3] As we examine the need in the church for a broader, more complete, and more extensive understanding of education, we realize that one way to understand it is as the fashioning of form. Education in the church means taking those forms which ecclesial life presents to us, places in our hands, as clay to be molded. Education is the work of lifting up and lifting out those forms through which we might refashion ourselves into a pastoral people.

Although it has not been a dominant strand, such a conception of education has been with us for some time in general education and more specifically in religious education.[4] John Dewey, for example, conceived of education as the *reconstruction* and *reorganization* of experience. Dewey not only taught that the work of education is a continuing and ongoing reorganization of experience which enables us to give meaning to the experience we have already had and to discover what meaning resides in our present experience. He also taught that reorganization—or refashioning—directs the course of subsequent experience.[5] To my mind, Dewey's choice of *reconstructing* and *reorganizing* immediately suggests the making, creating, designing, and *forming* nature of education.

More recently, in their work on models (which may be thought of as a particular kind of form), Joanmarie Smith and Gloria Durka have directed attention to form. In their teaching that education means the proposal of more and more adequate models of reality, they point out that educated persons are those whose lives—as complete entities from birth to death—are characterized by commitment to models capable of *shaping* those lives. In their work, they express reservations similar to those cited above, writing, "We are concerned that education is too often equated with the amount and breadth of skills and information one has mastered rather than the critical fidelity to adequate models."[6]

The most extensive exploration of formgiving in contemporary educational writing, however, and the one on which I base my own, is found in the work of Gabriel Moran. Moran teaches that education refers to the "reshaping of life's forms with end and without end." In this description, he plays on the richness in the term "end," which has the connotation of "meaning," by saying that education is a reshaping of life's forms with end—with purpose or meaning. At the same time, however, education is lifelong, ongoing and unceasing: it is "without end."[7]

Further, and most pertinent to the meaning of education I am offering here, Moran names the great life forms that all of us receive into our lives when we are born: the forms that shape the universal human values of community, work, knowledge, and wisdom. Among these he names the concrete forms of family, job, schooling, and leisure which do not exist in isolation but are in interplay with each other in the life of every one of us. These are the great yet ordinary universal forms to which and by which all of us are educated.[8]

Implications for the Church as Educator

We begin to realize the richness of education as formgiving when we return to the pastoral vocation and to the church as a people with a mission and a ministry. Following up the understanding of education as the artistic work of formgiving, and taking Moran's notion that education occurs in the interplay of forms of learning (e.g., family with schooling with job with leisure) rather than in the isolation of one form, we notice that the work of the church, its ministry, is a similar constellation of related forms.

As I noted in the Introduction, the church's educational ministry has been embodied and lived in five classical forms: didache, koinonia, kerygma, diakonia, and leiturgia. If we would educate *to* all of these forms, as well as *through* all of them, then attending only to any one of them—didache (schooling or teaching/instruction), or for that matter leiturgia (worship and prayer)—simply will not do.

Instead, the fullness of the pastoral vocation will demand that any ecclesial education must be one that educates:

• to koinonia (community and communion) by engaging in the forms of community and communion;
• to leiturgia (worship and prayer) by engaging in the forms of prayer and worship and spirituality;
• to kerygma (proclaiming the word of God) by attention to and practicing and incarnating the kerygma, "Jesus is risen," in the speech of our own lives, especially the speech of advocacy;
• to diakonia (service and outreach) by attention to our own service and reaching out to others, personally and communally, locally and globally;

• to didache (teaching and learning) by attention to the most appropriate forms of teaching and learning (including schooling) in our own communities.

Should any of these be left out as full partners in the educational work of ministry, should any of these be downplayed, should any of these be exalted to the denigration of others, we would not be able to educate fully. All are needed.

The understanding of education that I am advocating as foundation for curriculum will also assume that the forms of ministry are interrelated. Community, for example, will have elements of kerygmatic speech, of teaching, of outreach, and of prayer; worship will have elements of community, teaching, outreach, and prophetic speech. Teaching will necessarily incorporate elements of outreach, prayer, community, and kerygma. Just as we have discovered that as persons, to be is to be with, we will discover, similarly, that to be any one form of ministry is also to be with all the others. Only then can they be complete.

Education as Priestly, Prophetic, and Political

Seeing church education as an interplay of these great forms will also enable us to draw more fully on the heritage we have received from the past and on the deeply embedded traditional forms of the priestly, the prophetic, and the political. The heritage of scripture, tradition, the lives of our ancestors in the faith, creed, gospel, prayer, sacrament, and law is often taught better through worship or preaching than through classroom instruction. The tradition itself is handed on more fully when it is done in the midst of the people, the community, who are the tradition in their own persons. The life of prayer educates us most not when we read books about it but when we fall on our knees. The sacramental life nourishes us when we take part in baptizing, in confirming, and in coming together to the Table. In other words, incorporating all the forms of ministry into our educational lives enables us to make that education a *priestly* one: a work of remembering, hallowing, and blessing.

In addition, understanding education in the church as an interplay of all the forms of ministry also supports our *prophetic* vocation. For as a people, when we say the words of justice and do the work of justice, our speaking and doing are credible only if outreach and service are associated with the more inner-directed works of teaching, learning, and prayer. At the same time, outreach and service combined with prayer and study—with leiturgia and didache—ensure that the work of justice will be informed and careful, based on solid thought, serious scholarship, and intelligent probing. They can make us strong in the head as well as in the heart. Or, put another way, bringing all the forms of ministry into interplay with one another will enable us to ensure a prophetic educational ministry.

Third, an education that takes form seriously and sees education as continuing over a lifetime is, in Thomas Groome's beautiful phrase, an education of "pilgrims in time" and a truly "political activity." As Groome reminds us, "If education pretends to be a private or nonpolitical enterprise, it is treating us as beings 'out of time' rather than 'in time.' But such a pretense is just that—a pretension. Educational activity cannot be confined to some private sphere; [it is] eminently political."[9] Following what I have proposed above, with reference to the interplay of the forms of ministry, the inclusion of several forms can highlight this *political* dimension. By giving special attention to koinonia (community), kerygma (proclamation), and diakonia (reaching out and serving) with the societal and corporate element they necessarily imply, we can ensure that our educational ministry does not neglect the political.

A New Framework[10]

Taking form seriously involves us in a refashioning of frameworks. It leads us to ask what contextual meaning of education will serve best in developing the pastoral vocation in all of us, in contrast to the meanings of education from which we may be operating now. My own observation is that presently we are in a "between" time, a time when an older context or framework is being let go, while a new one is in the process of being born. New frameworks come or are coming into play especially where criticisms such as I voiced above have been taken seriously.

In an earlier framework, educational ministry could be considered as individuals and/or officials of a church instructing children to know the lore and obey the law of the church. In a newer one, the whole community is educating and empowering the whole community to engage in ministry in the midst of the world. When set next to one another, the old and new frameworks can be envisioned in such a way that the basic refashioning and reshaping emerges in four areas: agency, activity, participation, and direction.

	Former	*Present*
Agent	Individual and/or official	The whole community
Activity	Instructing and/or indoctrinating	Educating and empowering
Participants	Children	The whole community
Direction	To know the lore and obey the laws	To engage in ministry in the midst of the world

Agency

The agency of education in the church is changing. By "agent" I refer not only to the persons who are doing the actual work but also to those who are responsible for that work. In our time, a dramatic change seems to be taking place in this area. Understanding is growing on the part of church members that all are responsible for education, basically because they form a people. This is in marked contrast to a time when either *(a)* it was assumed that certain individuals, such as the Sunday school teacher, the Confraternity of Christian Doctrine instructor, the principal, the director of Christian education, the director of religious education, or even the local church's committee on education—and only those—were responsible for education; or *(b)* it was assumed that the pastor—and in some cases the bishop—was the official educator (especially teacher) in the church and that any persons doing the activities of education did so only as participants in, or by the extension of, the official's pastoral office or episcopal mandate rather than as their own vocation.

The shift most noticeable here is from individuals or officials as responsible agents to the whole community as responsible agent. The doers of education are the community as community, as well as those persons in the community specifically delegated by the community to do particular educational work, such as schoolteaching, designing worship, planning outreach programs, or engaging in advocacy on behalf of the community. The main effect of this shift is that individuals are beginning to understand themselves as executors of the will of the people as a whole and to realize they are not, as individuals, fundamentally responsible for the education occurring in the community. Such basic responsibility resides in the whole body of the church, the mystical body (1 Corinthians 12), the body politic. They are realizing that the church does not *have* an educational program; it *is* an educational program.

A less noticeable element in the shift, however, and therefore one to be emphasized is that as agency moves from individual persons, especially officials, to the whole community, we are not doing away with the former. Instead, we are situating them in a larger context, since the community is made up of parishioners and of appointed, elected, and ordained officials. But the latter are not equal to the community—instead, they are part of the wider group, which is a more extended and extensive body of people.

Activity

Understanding of the meaning of education is changing. Although it is dying hard, we are seeing the demise of the equation of "education" with "instruction" (often instruction in the form of indoctrination). This was the burden of my remarks in the earlier part of this chapter. We once saw education solely as giving instruction and, even more specifically, explicating doctrine and dogma, especially biblical doctrine and dogma (one meaning of indoctrination). Now we are in a time of movement toward a broader, more inclusive, and more complete understanding of what it means to educate.

Such education includes education to and by teaching, to and by worship, to and by community, to and by proclamation and prophetic speech, and to and by service. But a particular element that is growing in importance today is that the educating includes persons coming to understand their own gifts, their own talents, and their own powers. Education includes a recognition that we have received the grace of power.[11] Education is the community engaged in the move to recognize and develop this inner power and exercise it on behalf of the church and the gospel. This work of "empowering" is captured in a dialogue of Christopher Logue, where the summons "Come to the edge" initially draws the response "We might fall" or "It's too high." Eventually, however, the repeated invitation does bring the one called to the edge. When that occurs, the other—the educator—can push gently, and the one called, instead of falling, can learn to fly.[12] Education includes not only the calling and the listening to the call; it includes the coming, the pushing, and the flying.

It needs to be said, nevertheless, that educating does still include instructing and even—if a positive meaning such as "explicating doctrine" is admitted—indoctrinating. The major change is the realization that these are not the only activities included in the meaning of education. Just as individuals and officials are now set in the wider context of the community, so instruction and indoctrination are being set in the wider tasks of educating and empowering.

Participation

The participants in educational work are increasingly not only children but all in the community. Conferences and conventions devoted to all the forms of educational ministry draw persons of every age and every state of life not only nationally but internationally. The emerging laity continue to realize their need to be participants and to feel the effects of participation for their lives. At the local level, where the meanings of education have been broadened and the misunderstandings noted earlier have been addressed, a changed self-understanding resides in the people of the church. The realization is taking hold that education is indeed lifelong and that although it is work which necessarily includes children as participants, it is not exclusively devoted to children, nor should it be. The whole community as agent is, by its ways of living together, speaking together, praying together, and worshiping together, causing a shock of recognition in person after person that reveals them to themselves, saying, "I am being educated by and in this community to become who I am."[13]

Where are some of these participants coming to such understanding? At potluck suppers; on trips to Latin America with Witness for Peace; at their dinner tables and in their living rooms, whenever there are family devotions; at meetings of Parents Without Partners or of the newly widowed; at AA meetings; in soup kitchens; at the baptism of a new church member; during the weekly sermon; or in planning lessons for the fourth-graders—places that are familiar. In addition, self-understanding of oneself as in "continuing" education is also occurring at the work-places of the participants: selling clothing or used cars; operating a day-care center; managing a health-mainte-nance program for Blue Cross; driving a train or a truck; filling gas tanks or working on automobiles at a gas station; or bathing one's child. And not only those places. Self-understanding of oneself as a lifelong learner is also hap-pening to patients in hospitals and to friends drying the tears of friends who have faced tragedy; in sitting by the seaside as part of a vacation; in playing a game of tennis or basketball or golf; or in running or jogging. The whole community is coming to know itself as learner, to know itself as the subject of education, and to know itself as the one whose path is unending.

Direction

The direction of education is shifting. Where once it was agreed and assumed that the direction or purpose of education led to knowing the lore, through study and reading and listening, and to learning to obey the laws that embodied our code of morality, we see today that such direction makes sense only when set in the wider context of *what we do with* that knowledge and learning—of how we live it. And so, the direction in the framework now being fashioned is one where the whole community edu-cates the whole community *through* lore and law but *to* the pastoral vocation of engaging in ministry in the midst of the world.

Education, in other words, is toward the fashioning and refashioning of the life forms of ministry, as this people we are embodies them in the world. Knowing the lore and obeying the law of God are the heart of this work, but even they must be set in the larger context. For genuine educa-tion in the church is toward creating and living more and more adequately as religious beings in the world. Educa-tion is toward the continuing remaking, re-creating, reconstructing, and reorganizing of our human experience, giving that experience meaning and helping us decide where to go and what to do next. Education is in the direction of the call to world-aware ministry. That call is not only to life in the church. It is to life in the midst of the world within which the church itself dwells. It is to a ministry not bounded by church property lines or limited to the church building, although the ministry includes those places too. Rather, it is to a ministry where the only boundaries are those of the planet. The direction of education is the discovery that no place is God's "special" place, God's "only" place, for everywhere can be the place where the community meets God. No time is God's "special" time, for at every moment God's presence can be discovered. And no people are God's "special" people, for all people belong to God. Every place, every time, and every person is a lure from, and a lure to, the divine.

Such direction implies a broadened understanding of curriculum as well. In chapter 3 we turn our attention to that newer, broader meaning, examining curriculum as the entire course of the church's life.

REFLECTION AND PRACTICE

Exercise 1: Questions for Musing and for Discussion

1. What are three incidents in your life that educated you before you were fifteen?

2. What are three incidents in your life that educated you in your adult life?

3. What leads you to name these incidents as times when you were "educated"? In other words, what is your working meaning of education?

4. How many of these six incidents happened in school?

5. How many happened outside school?

6. Who were your teachers?

Exercise 2: Exploring Frameworks

1. Break into groups of three or four persons.

2. In each group, look at the two frameworks described in the last part of chapter 2.

3. Which of the two would you say is more descriptive of your local church? Why?

4. Are there different aspects of the framework (agent, activity, participants, direction) that are more developed than other parts?

5. After a half hour (or an agreed-upon time), bring your findings back to the whole group.

Exercise 3: Biblical Models for Ministry

In the scriptures, Mary, the mother of Jesus, is one who models all the forms of ministry in her life. She ponders the scriptures, she praises God in adoration and thanksgiving, she joins with others to wait for the Spirit, she exercises advocacy on behalf of a bridal couple, and she travels to assist her older cousin—study, prayer, community, kerygma, and outreach.

DIDACHE: Luke 1:29. "She . . . considered in her mind what sort of greeting this might be."

LEITURGIA: Luke 1:46–47. "My soul magnifies the Lord, and my spirit rejoices in God my Savior."

KOINONIA: Acts 1:12ff. "They returned to Jerusalem . . . and . . . went up to the upper room, where they were staying, . . with the women and Mary the mother of Jesus, and with his brothers."

KERYGMA: John 2:3–5. "When the wine gave out, the mother of Jesus said to him, 'They have no wine.' . . . His mother said to the servants, 'Do whatever he tells you.' "

DIAKONIA: Luke 1:39. "In those days Mary arose and went with haste" to visit her cousin Elizabeth.

Taking these biblical stories as examples, search for other persons in the Bible who model the forms of ministry. Bring their stories to the group, if you are working with a group, or to your own meditation, if you are searching the scriptures as a form of prayer.

Exercise 4: Ministry in Your Local Church

It is one thing to argue for more extensive understandings of educational ministry, as we have done in this chapter. It is another to determine where your local church or parish actually stands with reference to these issues. The following questionnaire takes much time and thought. It might serve as the basis for individual reflection, for an overnight staff or deacons meeting, or as the basis of parish meetings over a year-long period. This is an interesting questionnaire to administer according to age groups: for example, people under ten, ten to twenty, twenty to thirty, thirty to forty, etc.

The Questions

1. Does the parish need to be involved in the education of children? If so, what specific things should it do?

2. Does the parish need to be involved in the education of adolescents? If so, what forms should this take?

3. Does the parish need to be involved in the education of adults? If so, in what ways?

4. Does the parish need to be involved in social justice?

5. Does the parish need to be involved in problems of poverty, adequate housing for all its members, war, prison reform?

6. Does the parish need to be involved in influencing local, state, and federal legislation? If so, how?

The Allocation of Resources

Given the areas of need you chose for the parish tasks, how would you allocate parish financial resources on a percentage basis?

Given the areas of need you chose, how would you allocate parish personnel resources on a percentage basis?

Given the areas of need you chose, how would you allocate the resources of the physical plant of the parish on a percentage basis?

Making Decisions

Would you see any need for a revision of decision-making power in the parish if there were a consensus concerning revision of priorities in the parish?

What revisions would you suggest?

How might they be effected and implemented?

3

Curriculum: The Course of the Church's Life

My intention in this chapter is to explore the meanings of curriculum that follow from the pastoral and educational foundations presented in chapters 1 and 2. I will begin by examining some of the multiple meanings of curriculum existing today. Then I will look at five recent curricular challenges. Next, and working from these, I will offer an understanding of curriculum that is not so much new as it is a return to original sources. Finally, I will conclude with five principles, offering these as guides for future curriculum work.

Multiple Meanings of Curriculum

The word "curriculum" is derived from the Latin verb *currere,* which means to run.[1] In literal terms, a curriculum is a course to be run. In the institutional world of schooling, this literal notion of the course was metaphorically widened to "a course of study or training, as at a school or university," and used as early as 1633 at the University of Glasgow.[2] At the same time, curriculum as a term has been associated largely—and correctly, in my view—with the notion of "subject matter." Over the last century, although a substantial body of theory has developed around these two simple ideas (sometimes spoken of as process and content), no one definition of curriculum exists.[3] This is not to say that curriculum has *no* meaning. Rather, curriculum has multiple meanings, and in some instances the meanings are in conflict.

Central Concepts

Although it is more accurate—and fair—to say that most of the following meanings overlap, in some cases they nevertheless cluster around one or another central concept. Some of them focus on the concept of experience. Thus we have descriptions such as that of Howard Colson and Raymond Rigdon, who name curriculum as "the sum total of learning experiences in the local situation";[4] of Iris Cully, who points to it as "all learning experiences—the curriculum of life; the planned experiences in a learning environment; the materials and experiences derived from a course of study; a course of study";[5] and of William Pinar, who calls it "experience in educational contexts."[6]

Others will emphasize process, as does D. Campbell Wyckoff, who writes of curriculum as "a carefully devised channel of communication used by the church in its teaching ministry in order that the Christian faith and the Christian life may be known, accepted and lived."[7] Some will focus on environment, even one particular environment, as Gordon MacKenzie does in calling curriculum "the learner's engagements with various aspects of the environment which have been planned under the direction of the school."[8] Still others will bring together several of these elements, as do Arthur Lewis and Alice Miel, who call curriculum "a set of intentions about opportunities for engagement of persons-to-be-educated with other persons and with things (all bearers of information, processes, techniques, and values) in certain arrangements of time and space."[9]

Still another approach to the meaning of curriculum is that which takes aims, purposes, and context as the starting point and works with the notion that what you think curriculum *does* influences and determines what you think curriculum *is.* Thus, in the formulation of Elliot

Eisner and Elizabeth Vallance,[10] conflicting conceptions of curriculum follow from differing ends in view. The development of cognitive processes as end will assume that curriculum is that which develops literacy; a goal of practical and technical competence, or technological expertise, will focus on curriculum as procedures and know-how; self-actualization as a purpose will call forth a specifically human and humanistic course; and the goal of social reconstruction will call forth a focus that is global, societal, and political. What all these meanings hold in common, however, is the assumption that the curriculum develops in the context of the school—at least in part because of the emphasis in the United States on compulsory, universal schooling for all citizens.

Meanings in the Churches

Over the last hundred years the churches in the United States have developed their own meanings of curriculum, related to those cited above, but also in some ways distinct. Two events that happened within years of each other in the late nineteenth century shaped the meaning of church curriculum well into modern times. In Protestant circles, beginning in the 1880s, the first event was the devising of an all-Bible curriculum by Rev. John Vincent, who later became a Methodist bishop, and B. F. Jacobs, a Baptist layman. Ultimately, their dream of one course of study, to be used by every person in every Sunday school, from infant to the infirm, resulted in the Uniform Lesson Series, a standard series of lessons for Sunday schools with a list of scriptural topics presented regularly in yearly cycles, helpful guides for teachers, and a weekly Golden Text memory selection for pupils. Over a period of fifty-odd years, this became enormously successful and eventually was the accepted curriculum of evangelical Protestants throughout the Anglo-American world, lasting into the present time.[11]

In 1884 the Catholic Bishops of the United States, meeting in Baltimore, adopted not a uniform series of lessons

but a uniform catechism for Catholics, which was used
well into the period of Vatican II (1961–1965) and had a
similar effect. Memorization of the answers to such questions as "Why did God make you?" "What is forbidden by
the Seventh [or Fifth or First] Commandment?" and
"What are the names of the spiritual and corporal works
of mercy?" was a staple of intellectual fare for several
generations of U.S. Catholics. And although Catholics
were educated communally and liturgically by a broad
sacramental life, more powerful in many ways than the
catechism, it was the latter which was thought of as the
"curriculum" in Catholic education.

Actually, both Protestant and Catholic curricular practices in these instances were reflecting an assumption
stretching back to the Reformation and Catholic Counter-
Reformation. This was the implicit understanding that the
curriculum, or "what was taught," was taught from a
printed base—either the catechisms of Luther and his followers (or of the Catholic Counter-Reformation, especially
the Council of Trent) or the text of the Bible itself.

But whereas the reading of the Bible in the early centuries of Christianity had always occurred in the community
and as part of worship, as did the recitation of the creeds,
curriculum now began to exist as a text or as a set of texts
designed to help Christians know the lore and obey the
laws. This in turn led to the operating assumption that
curriculum was the printed material and nothing more.
And it had the reciprocal effect of creating a church whose
self-understanding of its educational vocation was the one
described in chapter 2: individuals and/or officials in
schooling contexts instructing children in knowledge and
behavior.

A shift in curriculum has become evident in recent
decades, however, one that is not so much new as a return
to the practice of centuries of church life, a practice never
entirely lost even with the invention of printing. As a
result of such tensions as those named in chapter 1—the
personal/communal, the local/global, and the clerical/lay
—as well as the new framework named in chapter 2,

churches are returning to the practice of seeing all the aspects of church life as educative and educating and thus part of curriculum. The next section will discuss specific examples from the last three decades that have challenged existing meanings and enabled the reclaiming of this wider meaning of curriculum, one that is reflective of an older, deeper, more biblical, and more communal tradition of Christianity.

Five Curricular Challenges

Many examples of contemporary, challenging influences might be cited as contributing to a reclaimed understanding of curriculum, but I will limit myself to five: two from general education and three from church education.

The first is a powerful essay by Fred Newmann and Donald Oliver. It attempted to "break the stranglehold by which the education profession has restricted our conception of education to structured activity carried on in school." Newmann and Oliver examined the powerful influence of "missing community" in most people's lives and suggested that the contexts for education were far too limited. They argued for at least three contexts: the school, the wider community, and the studio or work setting. They also consistently used metaphors such as reform, restructure, and reorganize—the importance for curriculum being the attention this gives to the reshaping of the entire environment affecting people's ordinary lives. As we noted above, environment is a major theme in curricular understandings today. They noted the limitations in the use of the term "extracurricular" for any environment outside of school (the seminar, the work setting, or a club to which people might belong). They advocated a broader educational context as the only one suitable for genuine learning, with the corollary curricular principle that what occurred in such contexts could and did constitute curriculum.[12]

A second example, presented under the direction of Ernest Boyer on behalf of the Carnegie Foundation for the

Advancement of Teaching, was the issuance of a report on
secondary schooling in the United States in 1983.[13] This
report advocated that in addition to schooling, students
should undertake a unit of service in the community of no
fewer than thirty hours each year. This unit would be
central to the curriculum and would in no way be considered "extracurricular." Similar to Newmann and Oliver,
those at the core of this proposal gave a meaning to curriculum as more extensive than what occurred in the one
form of school. Perhaps better, they made the point that
what occurred in the context—or form—of schooling was
enhanced when in interplay with all the experiences
found in additional contexts, notably those in the worlds
of work or service. To return to Pinar's meaning cited
above, "experience in educational contexts" includes the
contexts of work and community.

The third impetus for change came from the publication of *Christian Education: Shared Approaches (CE:SA)*,
by Joint Educational Development.[14] I cite this as an impetus toward change for several reasons. The timing is
one: the group of denominations that made up JED began
planning in the 1960s when the time for change was ripe;
the ecumenical approach—the corporate address to curriculum by the member denominations—is another; and
the importance of the Bible is a third. But for our purposes, the most important point to note concerning *CE:SA*
was its form.

The form of *CE:SA* was fourfold, with each form directed specifically to various elements of ministry. As a
form, *Knowing the Word,* for example, was a model of
didache—of teaching, of understanding, and of study from
printed texts. *Interpreting the Word,* in contrast, was, at
least in theory, as easily adaptable in situations of preaching (kerygma) and worship (leiturgia) as in the context of
schooling. *Living the Word,* as alternative and complementary to knowing and interpreting, was that form of
curriculum which could assist persons' maturing in faith as
they participated in the life and work of the Christian
community.[15] And *Doing the Word* was, as the term sug-

gested, directed to social concern in the local setting and beyond one's own boundaries: to diakonia.

In many ways, *CE:SA* fell short, especially where it focused these four forms, which were so rich in promise, on printed texts and stayed with what in practice continued to be schooling, especially in the curriculum guides offered. It also did not challenge the operative meaning of curriculum implicitly assumed through the great reliance on printed resources. On the other hand, it did provide a model cognizant of the diverse forms of educating in the church, which might still be the basis of a new approach to curriculum.

A fourth challenge lies in the reversal in curricular understanding brought about by Vatican II and by subsequent Catholic catechetical perspectives in the United States. The Vatican Council brought the Roman Catholic Church into a face-to-face position with the modern world and turned it away from its earlier posture of defense and apologetics. It stressed the liturgy, sacramental life, and engagement with the world as central for the Catholic Christian. The Council was a catalyst for revised catechetical thinking which necessarily went beyond the limiting form of the Baltimore Catechism. Although important for fundamental meanings and definitions, and as a pastoral reference and resource (its original usage), that catechism did not of itself extend to kerygma, leiturgia, diakonia, and koinonia. Finally, with the publication of *Sharing the Light of Faith,* the National Catechetical Directory for Catholics of the United States, a pattern for curriculum was proposed that directly included worship, advocated and expected social ministry, and was assumed to be lifelong, lasting through all the stages of human life.[16]

The fifth challenge—and here I situate myself—is that coming from religious educators aware of the limitation of present understandings of curriculum. This is a tradition extending as far back as the work of William Clayton Bower,[17] to whom I will return in chapter 9. I have already noted the work of Gabriel Moran, Joanmarie Smith, and Gloria Durka.[18] Two others who have pressed this issue

are John Westerhoff and C. Ellis Nelson. Westerhoff's formulation declaring the "schooling-instructional paradigm" bankrupt and suggesting instead a "community of
faith-enculturation" paradigm was an attempt to move to
the broader perspective I am advocating here.[19] On one
hand, it was unfortunate that schooling and community
were set in opposition rather than probed for their com-
plementarity. But on the other hand, few Christian religious educators have done more in actual practice to demonstrate how experiences in community and liturgy *are*
curriculum, in ways different from the content and processes of schooling.[20]

As for Nelson, the focus of much of his work is embodied
in *Where Faith Begins*, too rich a book to be summarized
here.[21] Nelson is most careful to distinguish printed curriculum from the whole curriculum, which he situates in the
life of the congregation, emphasizing that the starting
point is the congregation as the primary society of Christians and that life together is the method and the quality
of what is communicated. "The deliberate words and actions that parents and adults use in all kinds of specific
events and the quality of the corporate life of the believers
are curriculum."[22]

A Renewed Understanding of Curriculum

When we take all these factors into account—multiple
meanings, a changing ecclesial situation, and continuing
challenges to broaden curriculum—and draw on the many
strengths in the positions cited, what conclusions can we
draw at this time about the nature of curriculum? I propose three.

1. The meaning of curriculum is fluid; it is not set. Indeed, this is such a constant for anyone studying the field
of curriculum that James Gress and David Purpel's signif-
icant study can conclude, "A review of theory and research in curriculum reveals three persistent themes.
. . . (1) fundamental differences with respect to definitions
of curriculum, (2) theoretical versus practical pursuits, and

(3) the relative youth of the field itself."[23] What this might mean for us in the church is that we could be in the position, now, of uncovering new and varied meanings that could reconcile some of these differences; of arguing for the theoretical and the practical in interplay; and of understanding ourselves as co-creators of a still new field, a field that is aborning.

2. Church curriculum has always been broader than schooling alone, but today we are in the midst of recognizing and celebrating a meaning of curriculum that consciously incorporates other facets of ministry. The course to be run, the subject matter, is indeed "the sum total of learning experiences in the local situation." But it is also the "curriculum of life" beyond the local situation, already fashioned for us by centuries of church living which have created and re-created the diversity and the interplay of ecclesial forms, as well as encounter with the entire world. As we saw in the Introduction, this meaning is not new. Rather, it is a reiteration and a reincorporation of the first curriculum of the Christian people, stated in Acts 2:32, 42–47:

> This Jesus God raised up, and of that we all are witnesses [kerygma]. . . . And they devoted themselves to the apostles' teaching [didache; kerygma] and fellowship [koinonia], to the breaking of bread and the prayers [leiturgia]. . . . And all who believed were together and had all things in common [koinonia]; and they sold their possessions and goods and distributed them to all, as any had need [diakonia].

3. Given these two factors, we can conclude that a fuller and more extensive curriculum is already present in the church's life: in teaching, worship, community, proclamation, and outreach. Printed resources that serve this wider curriculum are in the treasury of the church, especially the comprehensive curricular materials designed over the last century in the United States. These, however, are not *the* curriculum. *The* curriculum is both more basic and more profound. It is *the entire course of the church's life,* found in the fundamental forms of that life. It is the

priestly, prophetic, and political work of didache, leiturgia, koinonia, kerygma, and diakonia. Where education
is the fashioning and refashioning of these forms in interplay, curriculum is the subject matter and processes that
make them to be what they are. Where education is the
living and the fashioning, curriculum is the life, the substance that is fashioned.

In the five chapters that follow I will attempt to be very
specific in illustrating some of the ways in which institu-
tionally we can imagine, fashion, and embody this broad
understanding of curriculum. I will offer some direction in
planning, designing, and forming it. In concluding this
chapter, however, I offer five educational principles to
guide us in this work.

Five Principles of Curriculum Design

*Principle 1: As church people, we must consistently dis-
tinguish between the curriculum of education and the
curriculum of schooling.* The distinction between the curriculum of education and the curriculum of schooling is
rarely made. Although many definitions of curriculum will
speak of all of life's experiences as part of curricular work,
the implicit assumption in almost everything written and
taught about curriculum is that, like education, it is in
practice limited to what adults do to and with children in
a place called a school. Even when curricular resources
are specifically planned for adults, they will tend to use a
schooling form.

Making a distinction between a curriculum of education
and a curriculum of schooling, however, could enable us
to break out of this limited and limiting meaning of curriculum. The distinction is actually quite simple. A curriculum of education will refer to the interplay of the several
forms through which education occurs—it will refer to
education in, to, and by service, community, proclamation, worship, and teaching. In contrast, a curriculum of
schooling will be a reference to only one of the many
valuable forms through which education occurs, that form

which generally happens in a place called a school, a form focused on processes of instruction, reading of texts, conceptual knowledge, and study.[24]

This simple distinction is easy to *think* when we focus on it. But our thinking makes little difference unless the distinction is actually used—regularly and pervasively. We will not really change curricular meanings until we start speaking in different ways. To know that education is more than schooling is not enough. We must learn to *say* "education" when we are referring to all the life forms that do educate: family, sports, work, and worship. We must learn to say "schooling" as well, when we are referring to that one form of education, and not use the generic term in reference to it. And if we are people whose life-work is the design and implementation of curriculum, especially if we are curriculum writers, we must express this distinction in everything we publish. Doing that could bring about a change that most of us desire: a broadened and enriched claiming of the pastoral vocation to which all of the church's life does in fact educate us. The alternative, as I have already been at pains to point out, is giving over the word "education" to only one of its forms, schooling, which does hidden but nonetheless extensive damage to the outcomes we desire as Christian educators.

Principle 2: The curriculum of educational ministry is multiple. Insisting on the distinction just described allows us to claim as educational forces all the forms of church ministry. Not only will Bible studies, catechesis, the pastor's class, and adult schooling sessions be seen as part of the educational enterprise. So too will the range of worship, prayer, and liturgical experiences which teach, instruct, and shape us in their own distinctive ways and are the subject matter of leiturgia in ways analogous to books and texts in schooling. So too will the rhythms of community life—among ourselves as families and church members, with other Christian groups, with people of other religions—rhythms where the curriculum of education is constituted by community life itself.

But this multiple nature of educational ministry will also

be manifest in our work and service lives and in the causes we choose to advocate. Ideally, we will come to discover, in envisioning educational ministry as multiple and manifold, that we are continually being educated throughout our lives and that when education stops, we stop. And when this inclusive educational experience begins to dawn upon us, we will also learn that the forms of education are not separate from one another. We will begin to see, for example, the community and advocacy dimensions in all schooling; the outreach and prayer needed by all advocacy and prophetic speech; and the instructional value and impetus to healing society in all prayer and worship. We shall also see, and celebrate too, that the church is, among societal institutions, ahead of most other institutions in being a key place where the understanding of education as multiple can flourish.

Principle 3: Subject matter has many layers. In speaking of curriculum, it is impossible to avoid the term "subject matter," and I have already used it several times in this chapter. Each form of the curriculum of educational ministry has its own distinct subject matter. But the point I wish to make here is that the term hides an equivocation. To quote William Walsh:

> On the one hand any subject matter is a system of clues, concerned with human existence organized about some initiating and defining concept [liturgy, service, community, proclamation, and teaching] expressed in language and argued by human beings. On the other hand, subject matter is that world of meaning, order of nature, physical process, pattern of events, organization of feelings which the former kind of subject matter enables us to conceive. It is that labyrinth of reality through which and towards which any particular discourse is a directing and guiding thread.[25]

Walsh concludes by asserting that unless subject matter in the first sense leads us to understand subject matter in the second sense, it fails to serve its purpose. And the reason for offering this issue as a principle of curriculum design is that the double meaning is rarely present in such design. My own belief is that such an absence is inevitable if the meaning of curriculum is limited to procedures and methods designed to present subject matter in the first sense, that is, if subject matter is assumed to be the system of clues and nothing more.[26]

If the many-layered richness of subject matter is taken as a principle, however, it expands and deepens the meaning of curriculum. It also leads to uncovering a third meaning. This is the understanding of human beings as subjects, as subjects who matter, in ways taught by the great Brazilian educator Paulo Freire. Freire believes that for human beings the essential decision is between speaking or remaining embedded in a culture of silence, between naming ourselves or being named by others, between remaining an object or becoming a subject. The heart of his vision is that every human being has an ontological vocation to be a subject, namely, someone who can separate from the world in his or her own consciousness, be critical of it, act on it, and transform it—in the process making the world a subject too.[27] Such a rich conception of "subject matter" can only further renewed curricular understanding, as we come to understand it as including not only the subject matter of every form of church life. It includes also the human subjects who *are* the church, the people being fashioned through the artistic and creative works of education and curriculum design.

Principle 4: The curriculum must be priestly, prophetic, and political. Such broadened meaning and expression of curriculum will need to be in relation to and informed by the past; it cannot be ahistorical. It will need to be based on an examination of the changing forms of ministry which have brought us into our own times, as well as being open to the discovery that ministry has an extensive history of different emphases. In some eras, ministry has been mainly cultic, at others juridical, and at still others prophetic or pastoral or monastic.[28] The forms we have received have been given us by people who also had a pastoral vocation—the people who are our tradition and who cannot be dismissed. In other words, the curriculum must be characterized by the priestly work of remembering.

But this work, in turn, needs to be in interplay with the work that still needs to be done. Our teaching, community, outreach, proclamation, and service must be continually rephrased and re-formed in the light of the demands the present makes. Our history of forgetting (pogroms, persecutions, perjuries,) as well as of remembering will have to be addressed. This is especially true when we consider ourselves as local bodies related to a world and to a world church. It is even more true as we directly address the plight of the refugees, orphans, and widows of our century and of the oppressed native peoples of other centuries—even as Jeremiah did, as Mary did, and as Isaiah did. In other words, each of the multiple forms of curriculum must have a prophetic dimension.

That in turn means that our curricular work must be involved with systems and structures, with policy and planning. It must be shaped and reshaped according to norms that engage all the people as teachers and as learners—the whole community educating the whole community, locally and worldwide, and in doing so, fashioning itself as a people. It must have its own laws, its own polity, its own communal forms for exercising, legislating, and sharing power. As we design it, the curriculum we create must be in touch with political realities, both within and beyond the church.

Principle 5: The curriculum must take into account three forms: the explicit curriculum, the implicit curriculum, and the null curriculum. In *The Educational Imagination,* Elliot Eisner points out that all institutions teach not one but three curricula.[29] The explicit curriculum refers to what is actually presented, consciously and with intention. It is what we say we are offering, what is found in our table of contents, or in church bylaws or pastoral constitutions.

The implicit curriculum, in contrast, refers to the patterns or organization or procedures that frame the explicit curriculum: things like attitudes or time spent or even the design of a room; things like the presence or absence of teenagers on our parish councils; or things like the percentage of church revenues we give or do not give to people who are less fortunate. Within the curriculum of community, for example, in a church that has a drama group, the explicit curriculum might be that the group is presenting *Godspell.* The implicit curriculum might be the circumstances that lead to casting: who gets what part; the confidence or lack of confidence of the performers; the personality of the director; whether all the major parts are for men or, for that matter, for women.

The null curriculum is a paradox. This is the curriculum that exists because it does not exist; it is what is left out. But the point of including it is that ignorance or the absence of something is not neutral. It skews the balance of options we might consider, alternatives from which we might choose, or perspectives that help us see. The null curriculum includes areas left out (content, themes, points of view) and procedures left unused (the arts, play, critical analysis). The implicit curriculum, in contrast, does not leave out areas and procedures. It simply does not call them to attention. They are there, operative in the situation but left unnoticed.

The design and preparation of church curricula, forms of education other than schooling—worship, community, prophetic speech, and outreach—often become the null curricula. They are left out of our concepts and understandings. Or, at best, they are left implicit, not spoken of or paid attention as part of the educational process. Similarly, two-way dialogue, extensive consultation of church members, and participation in decisions by all concerned may be among the processes that form the null curriculum.

To these three curricula, local churches attempting to offer the full range of education need to pay heed. As the church curriculum broadens from the curriculum of schooling to the curriculum of education and educational ministry, the whole church needs continuing awareness not only of what is consciously planned but of what is said in what is said and of what goes on in what goes on. The whole church needs continuing awareness, too, of what is *not* said and of what does *not* go on. The whole church needs to be both more discerning and more sophisticated in naming what is intuited, demonstrated, or conveyed, even when that is not at all what is intended. The whole church needs to realize that its curricular vocation is a confrontation with life—the entire life of the church, manifest in both subtle and not so subtle ways. And as the church comes to such realization, it can turn its more direct attention to the extraordinary vocation to which it is called. This will be the burden of the five chapters that follow.

REFLECTION AND PRACTICE

Exercise 1: Questions for Musing and for Discussion

1. As you look over the many definitions of curriculum given at the beginning of this chapter, which one most characterizes the understanding of it that prevails in your local church?

2. What are its advantages?

3. What are its disadvantages?

4. What meanings of curriculum suggested in this chapter are, in your view, most important for the future of the church?

5. If you could change one thing about your local church curriculum, what would it be? Why?

6. If you could keep one thing about your local church curriculum, what would it be? Why?

Exercise 2: The Three Curricula
Your Church Teaches

This exercise is done in a group.

Divide the group evenly into three subgroups. Each group is to consider a different form of curriculum: the explicit, the implicit, and the null.

After being sure the meanings of each of the curricula are clear to each person, each group is to spend forty-five minutes responding to the following:

- What are three examples of the explicit (implicit, null) curriculum in our church?
- What is "taught" by each of these examples?
- Is what is "taught" in harmony with what is assumed or expected by the whole community?
- What is explicit (implicit, null) in our procedures and methods as a church, our processes and ways of doing things: in teaching; in worship; in community; in advocacy, word, prophetic speech; and in outreach.

Exercise 3: Examining Our Printed Resources

This exercise is especially designed for a curriculum committee or education committee (or director of religious education, director of Christian education, pastoral associate) responsible for buying printed materials.

Copy from at least five sources (textbooks, teacher's manuals, encyclopedias, dictionaries, church documents) the definition for curriculum.

Select at least five articles in either church or secular educational journals. Notice how the word "curriculum" is used, or what meaning is implied, in these journals. Do the same thing for the word "education."

If your own meaning is changing as a result of this chapter or as a result of this research, restate it.

If you are doing this work in a group, pool your definitions.

Exercise 4: Clarifying Our Purposes

In chapter 2, the purpose of education was described as *(a)* knowing the lore and obeying the law and *(b)* engaging in ministry in the midst of the world. In this chapter, four purposes of curriculum were noted: literacy, technology, self-transcendence, and social reconstruction.

This exercise is a group exercise. Divide into five groups, with each taking a different form of ministry: didache, koinonia, leiturgia, kerygma, and diakonia.

- What are five ways your congregation is educated to and by this form?
- What are the explicit or implicit purposes that each of these forms therefore suggests?
- In what ways are these in harmony—or disharmony— with the purposes of educational ministry?

PART TWO

THE
VOCATION

4

Koinonia:
The Curriculum
of Community

I move now to the first of the curricular forms, koinonia. The pattern of the chapter, as well as of the four that follow, will be this: After suggesting several central meanings for the particular ministry, I will focus on the major forms each ministry takes. After that I will explore some of the curricular tasks within the form. Then, as in chapters 1 to 3, I will conclude with exercises for reflection and practice. In no section, however, will I be presenting a finished plan or a complete study. Rather, each chapter and each section of the chapter is designed as a blueprint: basic, exploratory, and catalyst for readers' own work with others in curriculum, as well as for decisions based on their communal experience.

Meanings of Community

In choosing to begin with koinonia, rather than with teaching or worship, I am proposing community and communion as the initial educational ministry. Often the first curricular move is to choose subject matter for the activity of teaching and then to zero in immediately on what instructors might do and which materials they might use. That is a critical task and not to be minimized. But for precisely that reason I wish to highlight the necessity of community as starting point in educational ministry. Only

out of life together as a people do patterns of worship or
programs for teaching or outreach make sense. The fashioning of a people does not occur unless a people exists to
be fashioned.

People come into church communities in many different ways, and often in a combination of ways. Some find
themselves in a particular neighborhood and either accept
or search out the nearest local congregation. Others look
for a faith community with an ethos, a particular angle of
vision or attitude as a church, and test out a congregation
by visiting it several times before making a choice. Others
are born into a particular church setting and throughout
their lives are formed as Baptists or Catholics or Presbyte-
rians to such a degree that it is part of their personal
identity. Still others ask friends or neighbors whether they
know of a church that might meet their needs. And still
others choose a church home that is compatible not only
with their personal desires, beliefs, and conviction but also
with their corporate needs as a family, giving important
consideration to the congregation's care for children.

But the common elements in affiliating with a community tend to be remarkably constant. These are the impetus toward belonging; toward associating with those sharing a common heritage, belief, and way of life; and toward
the human need to share. Although it may not be reached,
the ideal embodied in community is the movement
toward unity and union with others: *comm*unity and
*comm*union. Deep within the human heart is a longing for
a holy time when "all will be one," a dream of a new
heaven and a new earth where death shall be no more,
neither shall there be mourning nor crying nor pain any-
more. In that new heaven and new earth, God will wipe
away every tear from our eyes (Revelation 21). This, ultimately, is the undersong of every joining.

In somewhat different language, people seek out a place
where love is the root. Contemporary society talks little
about love, although continuing to hunger for it. That is in
rather direct and stark contrast with the Gospel of John:
"God so loved the world" (John 3:16); "This is my com-

mandment, that you love one another as I have loved you" (John 15:12); and with the letters of John: "For this is the message which you have heard from the beginning, that we should love one another" (1 John 3:11; "And now I beg you . . . that we love one another" (2 John 1:5); "God is love, and they who abide in love abide in God, and God in them" (1 John 4:16, alt.). The poet, W. H. Auden, puts the teaching this way: "We must love one another. We must love one another or die."

Such is the burden of Christian community: to become a people "rooted and grounded in love," with the power "to comprehend with all the saints what is the breadth and length and height and depth, and to know the love of Christ which surpasses knowledge, that we may be filled with all the fulness of God" (Eph. 3:17–19). Indeed, love has been the burden of community from the beginning and therefore the core of the ministry of koinonia: the ministry of community and communion. As the word signifies, this is the ministry that moves us toward the healing of division, toward overcoming brokenness, and ultimately toward achieving wholeness. One Christian is no Christian; we go to God together or we do not go at all. In terms of fashioning a people, this works by giving us three aspects of community: as governing reality; as convicting reality; and as as-yet-unrealized and incomplete reality.

Community as Governing Reality

In a worship setting, whenever we recite the Apostles' Creed together we acknowledge the fundamental power of community as governing reality in the Christian life: "I believe in . . . the communion of saints." Although we may reflect on it only rarely, the truth of Christian community is that whenever we acknowledge our relatedness, either implicitly or explicitly, we contribute our share to the building up of the present, living body of the Christ, to the fashioning of that people who are the community of Jesus. In addition, the doctrine of the communion of saints reminds us that this body stretches centuries into the past and is the way we have of keeping faith with the dead, with the tradition.

The communion of saints, doctrinally, constitutes us as a people. It makes us who we are at the same time that it binds us to our heritage. G. K. Chesterton reminded us of this bonding many years ago. In *Orthodoxy*, he wrote that tradition "may be defined as an extension of the franchise. Tradition means giving votes to the most obscure of all classes, our ancestors. . . . Tradition refuses to submit to the small and arrogant oligarchy of those who merely happen to be walking about."[1]

The communion of saints also binds us to the future. The prophetic impulse involves living fully *in the present* out of our responsibility to the future—to our children and our children's children. We keep faith with the future by recognizing our communion with those yet to be born. In John Westerhoff's formulation, we are a community of memory, of vision, and of hope.[2] Although all three are sedimented in our souls, we the living are the ones who fashion the future vision, chastened by memory and buoyed up by hope.

One warrant for the fashioning is, as we have already seen, scriptural: "Thou shalt love." But another warrant toward community is theological. For the touchstone and ultimate symbol of communion is a divinity who from the first centuries has been presented to us as a community of Persons. Thomas Aquinas writes that what is in common possession by these persons is their very being or existence.[3] Community makes God to be what God is. And although trinitarian understanding has been opened to new images such as Creator, Redeemer, and Sustainer —paradoxically reminding us that God is beyond all imagery—the idea that God is community remains because it resonates so deeply within us. The symbol of community is not only of the Divinity. Because we are created as human beings in the image of God, it also is ours, also is us—at least as desired dream and hoped-for destiny. We too are called to be a community of persons, and the way we fashion ourselves in this ministry—koinonia—is born, lives, and rises out of the heart of the mystery of God.

Community as Convicting Reality

To a great extent, if we did not have scripture, theology, creed, and tradition to remind us of community and to anchor us there as people, we would probably invent them. Community—the move toward wholeness, unity, and union—is so powerful a lure as to be a necessity. We know this from examining, first, our own inner experience: the feelings we so often have of estrangement, of lostness, of being outsiders. The periodic loss of equilibrium that constitutes our human condition is the continuing reminder of our passion for completeness and at-onement within as well as beyond ourselves.

But the lure of community and the experience of separation is felt just as deeply in our human impulse to go out to others: from infancy, where we take in the other with our eyes, then our bodies, and then our speech; to childhood, where we are filled with the thirst to know not only ourselves but our surroundings and our world; to adulthood, where we search for intimacy and affection and friendship on one level and for connectedness and the breaking down of barriers and the healing of global division on the other. Albert Camus captured both the lure toward and the estrangement from community:

> The first progressive step for a mind overwhelmed by the strangeness of things is to realize that this feeling of strangeness is shared with all . . . and that human reality, in its entirety, suffers from the distance which separates it from the rest of the universe. The malady experienced by a single man or woman becomes a mass plague. In our daily trials rebellion plays the same role as does the *"cogito"* in the realm of thought: it is the first piece of evidence. But this evidence lures the individual from his or her solitude.[4]

In our own time, we feel this lure in two areas we had apparently forgotten. These are the impulses (1) toward

land and other animals, air and water, earth and fire: the
nonhuman creation which has so often been shut out of
the human community; and (2) toward understanding the
peoples of cultures far different from our own. To put it
in religious language, we are "convicted" of our vocation
to community simply by living a human life.

Community as a Not-Yet-Realized Reality

In our conviction, we are brought up short. At the same
time we are drawn to community, we find ourselves surrounded by bruised and broken community or by the absence of any community at all. Apartheid, violence, war.
Sexism, racism, ageism. Terror in the streets and terror in
the home. Abuse in the White House and abuse in the
house next door. The rent and bleeding garment of the
body of the Christ, still torn by the enmity and hatred and
bitterness of centuries. Beyond that: Christian killing Muslim and Muslim killing Christian. Ireland. Beirut. India.
Wounded Knee. Auschwitz. If we are at all sensitive, at all
touched by the gospel of Jesus, these circumstances bring
us to our knees and to the position of listeners. For community is not yet realized. Often, the educational impulse
moves us at such moments as we recognize the relation
between community and other ministries. With prayer,
where on our knees we ask, "O God, what would you have
us to do?" And with teaching, prophetic speech, and outreach, where, we suspect, some of the answers may lie.

But before directly addressing these other ministries, let
us examine the basic forms that community takes in the
church as well as the curricular tasks that community demands as we work educationally toward its formation and
re-formation.

Forms of Community

The church today has already moved into the position
of listening—not everywhere, but certainly in enough
situations—to such a degree that we are beginning to

gather new evidence and new understanding as to how we might educate toward community in our time. This is particularly evident in the willingness of churches throughout the world, and even here at home, to rethink, reshape, and redesign our ways of coming together and being together as people in community: to reshape and redesign our forms of community.

The proliferation of house churches and of basic Christian communities are two examples. Youth churches, gay congregations, and movements such as WomanChurch are others.[5] Indeed, sometimes house churches and basic Christian communities are different terms for the same thing: small groups of people, with or without an ordained leader, coming together in their homes to reflect on the scripture and its relation to their own lives, their work, their families, and their societies.

Nevertheless, the basic forms of Christian community, here in the United States as we come to the end of this century, continue to be *the local parish* and *the family.* If the subject matter of community is as we have just described, if education is the fashioning and refashioning of form, and if curriculum is the substance of the experience we have in these forms, what curricular tasks do the parish and the family present for today's Christian people? I suggest three as critical for each. For the parish, the tasks are inclusion, leadership, and outreach. For the family they are presence, receptivity, and responsibility. Learned in these settings as the core of the forms themselves, they can eventually be brought to bear on all our relations in the world, and to all the communities in which we participate. They can contribute to our finally realizing the as-yet-incomplete reality.

Parish: Curricular Tasks

1. *Inclusion.* As a curricular task, inclusion exists on several levels. The first refers to the way a local church takes into account the fact that while its members will have different perspectives on what it is to be church, it

has to have room for them all. For example, every church has traditional members for whom the church is essential; involved members for whom the church is central; contemporary members for whom the church is privileged— or special—(although neither essential nor central); and independent members for whom the church is valuable.[6] Such divergent points of view on church and by extension on gospel, doctrine, and orthodoxy must not only be recognized but also appreciated as sincere positions. Holding one or another ought not to make persons feel unwelcome.

Another facet of inclusion has to do with those who feel isolated. A recent study of parish life in the United States indicates several groups who might be perceived, or perceive themselves, as not really included: traditionalists, singles, newcomers, cliques that formerly dominated church life and no longer do, those alienated by church response to divorce, and ethnic or racial minorities.[7] The study does not mention those alienated because of a church's position on homosexuality or its attitudes toward women, but for most churches, these would certainly need to be noted too.

Ironically, one of the groups named above, singles, may feel alienated because they are surrounded by a church that constantly uses family metaphors in both theology and parish life; are located in parishes that often list membership by family units; worship in liturgies whose hymns, responses, and sermons reinforce family images; and observe the great disproportion in parish programs and activities directed to people in some stage of family life rather than to singles. The irony here is that often the imagery and stress on family can obscure many alternate forms of family too, such as persons outside the mother-father-children imagery—an obscurity that may cause many families to feel alienated, or not included.

The response to experiences of alienation are of course manifold. But any local parish can consciously respond to the absence of inclusiveness by attending to language, programs, and forms of greeting. Simple practices such as acknowledging and gathering people before and after services; using imagery other than, or in addition to, family imagery (especially about itself as a "church family"); visitation to new members regularly; monthly meetings for alienated or "former" Christians (including singles); and committees and communities of "hospitality" who make it their business to know about, and then do something in response to, loneliness, illness, birth, suffering, and death in persons' lives—all can go a long way toward meeting these needs.

2. *Leadership.* Despite the many new forms of church now being born and the shifting meanings of "clergy" and "laity" noted in chapter 1, it remains true that the most visible and most influential person in any parish is the pastor. The pastoral office and the way it is exercised have profound influence on persons' attachment to parish and their sense of community.[8] This has meaning not only for the particular pastor, who, seeking to foster community, must try to know the names and cares of all parishioners. It has meaning as well for looking at proposals to make individual parishes communities of communities where peoples' names are known. In practice, such proposals may lead to dividing the parish into smaller units that at times function on their own yet still come together regularly with the larger group. This allows everyone to experience leadership, not so much individually but as a group responsible for itself and to the larger community. And from another perspective, it also has implications for seminary education and the degree of importance an individual seminary gives to pastoral and parish leadership, including the emphasis on and quality of field education, the opportunities for varied human engagements, and the ability to keep an open mind.

The other dimension of leadership contributing to community is the extent and variety of leadership exercised by the laity in local parish life. This refers not only to boards of deacons, parish councils, and paid employees on parish staffs. It refers even more to the presence of church members in pastoral and decision-making situations, in carry-

ing on the work of the parish (from keeping accounts to
fixing plumbing), and in experiencing themselves as
needed and necessary to the parish. Articulating this vision, some church bulletins list as ministers in the church,
"Everybody." And in *The Christian Parish,* Pastor William Bausch gives an example of laity's leadership, in the
form of pastoral care. Bausch recalls:

> A few years ago a woman who had a mastectomy told me
> that, having gone through it both physically and emotion-
> ally, she would be glad to talk to any woman who was faced
> with the same problem. From this I began to ask various
> people who had and were suffering from other problems if
> they would be willing to do the same. Even more, would
> they allow their names and phone numbers to be put in the
> parish booklet? They would, and so in our one-to-one minis-
> try we have people who know from personal experience:
> alcoholism, homosexuality, amputation, brain-damaged
> children, death of a child, cancer, job loss, heart attack,
> depression, divorce, chronic illness, and the like. These peo-
> ple are "wounded healers."[9]

3. *Outreach.* Rev. Philip Murnion, who directs the National Pastoral Life Center in New York City, argues that
parish as community is not only a product of hospitality
and friendliness. Parish also comes from feelings of rooted-
ness. Where loss of community comes when common
faith, worship, and life are lacking, the recovery of community comes from clearly proclaiming faith, gospel, and
social justice. But even then, Murnion argues, dialogue
about faith and justice for any community must lead to
that parish embracing it as *their* faith, *their* justice. Rather
than through a curriculum of schooling, such dialogue
takes the form of a curriculum of community, actions that
share grief as well as joy. These happen when a parish
community tries to come up with collateral to stave off
foreclosure on a farm family; when it supplies food, clothing, and shelter for a burned-out family; when it unites
with other churches in establishing a center for AIDS victims, or hospices for the dying, or homes for pregnant,
unwed teenagers; or when it offers itself as sanctuary for

political refugees.[10] To name outreach as a facet of the curriculum of community is simply to proclaim that community is taught by the way it is lived. It is also to proclaim that the great forms of educational ministry (in this case community and outreach) can never be totally separate in practice.

Family: Curricular Tasks

In the past two decades, several fine volumes have examined the ways family as community educates. In passing, I want to pay tribute to such resources as *Parenting for Peace and Justice; Raising Good Children; How to Help Your Child Have a Spiritual Life;* and *Family Ministry.*[11] For persons seeking in-depth examination of the curriculum of community applied to the form of family, such volumes are invaluable. However, my intention here is different from those fine works. Here I am naming the curricular tasks that comprise the components of the koinonia curriculum in the context of the family. This curriculum is not in reading books but in acting in very specific ways. The curriculum in the family is of course different from that of the parish. A family educates to community, not by being a local church, but by being a family and by doing what a family does. It educates to community by being a community, an especially intimate community. Three essential elements constitute family life: presence, receptivity, and responsibility. The family is the basic laboratory where these human qualities educate, shape, and fashion persons' lives.

1. *Presence.* In order to be in community with other people, we ourselves need to have a sense that we are subjects, human subjects (not objects), who participate in existence. But we do not have a sense of our own subjectivity unless other people mirror it back to us. It is not enough to see ourselves, we must see other people seeing us, which is to say appreciating, valuing, and cherishing. The way they do this is through human presence.

All of us know enough to realize that community does

not exist merely because one person stands next to another or is physically present to another. We have all had
the experience of feeling completely alone in a crowd. But
when another is humanly present to us, we are deeply
aware of it. The great philosopher of presence, Gabriel
Marcel, describes it this way:

> It is an undeniable fact, though it is hard to describe in
> intelligible terms, that there are some people who reveal
> themselves as "present"—that is to say at our disposal.
> There is a way of listening which is a way of giving, and
> another way of listening which is a way of refusing, of refus-
> ing oneself. The material gift, the visible action do not nec-
> essarily witness to presence. . . . Presence is something
> which reveals itself in a look, a smile, an intonation or a
> handshake.[12]

The family is the setting where such presence can be offered and received, where personal subjectivity can be
claimed, and where the capacity for communion can be
nourished as a result. It is the place where we are given
our names. Therefore, in the family, all the activities that
cultivate assisting the other as coming to self-understanding can contribute to presence: family meetings where all
speak and are listened to; special outings by parents with
a particular child on her or his birthday; moments together in the bath with very small children; viewing
videos together; taking care to celebrate family, religious,
or national holidays; and rituals at meals and at the beginning and the ending of each day.

2. *Receptivity.* At least in some sense, the other side of
presence is receptivity. This implies the readiness to listen
to the entire creation addressing us, and ultimately to the
Creator Spirit reaching out to be present to us. It is a
reminder that before we respond to creation, we first must
listen to it and hear it. Receptivity is expressed in the
poet's prayer, "Teach us to care and not to care; teach us
to sit still," and in the wise old folk saying, "Sometimes ah
sets and thinks; and sometimes ah jes sets." Receptivity
means bringing our contemplative powers to bear on

whatever reality lies before us—whether person or thing —and facing that reality as a "Thou."

Among the most important aspects of receptivity is hospitality: receiving others as they are. To quote Marcel again:

> If we devote our attention to the act of hospitality, we will see at once that to *receive* is not to fill up a void with an alien presence but to make the other participate in a certain plenitude. Thus the ambiguous term "receptivity" has a wide range of meanings extending from suffering or undergoing to the gift of self; for hospitality is a gift of what is one's own, that is, of oneself.[13]

The family, because it is a primary place of suffering and undergoing as well as a place of joy and celebration, is in the unique position to give to human beings one of the first experiences of receptivity: receptivity to themselves. Parents who are aware of this need on the child's part understand that full community will not be possible, not with the mutuality and interdependence it implies and calls for, unless all family members listen to themselves, are receptive to themselves, and are *delivered to* themselves. Such parents know that receptivity to ourselves is an essential condition for wider communion. And the place where we nurture and cultivate this receptivity is in the company of those with whom we come to understand our humanity: the company of our own families.[14]

3. *Responsibility.* This follows from presence and receptivity. When others in both human and nonhuman creation address us—and when above all the Other addresses us—the fully human call is to response. "The human being's central characteristic is to respond or to answer."[15] And as we begin to do this, from infancy on guided by our parents and other family members—especially as we watch what they do—we begin developing the moral capacity to be in responsible relation to all that is.

The educating of this capacity for responsibility has for too long been relegated to the schools and to the sermon during worship. These two are appropriate places only if they are in touch with the fundamental setting where education in responsibility takes place. And that setting is, of course, the family, where each new person and new thing the child meets calls forth from the child some kind of answer. "There was a child went forth every day," wrote Walt Whitman, "And the first object he look'd upon, that object he became, / And that object became part of him for the day or a certain part of the day, / Or for many years or stretching cycles of years."[16]

The curricular task of the family in this instance is both particular and practical. It involves *(a)* awakening and assisting the child in her or his meetings with creation— creating zones of awareness and quiet as much as is necessary and, most of all, taking time; *(b)* taking seriously its role of educating toward responsibility in cooperation with other ministries such as teaching and worship; and *(c)* distinguishing for the child between being responsible *to* and being responsible *for*. Often, children as well as adults are confused by this distinction—thinking they are responsible *for* everything and everyone, while believing they are responsible *to* very few. Actually the opposite is the case. Human beings are responsible *for* ourselves and our actions from earliest childhood—although in the beginning we need help in coming to realize this—while we are responsible *to* all creation. Such learning can be fostered in the family when children are given opportunities, through care for pets and plants and pots and pans, to grow toward greater responsibility *for* themselves in the journey toward adulthood, while learning that the moral vocation in life is to be responsible *to* all things and all people.

> Our confusion about what we are responsible *for* is tied to our failure to ask the prior question: What are we responsible *to?* The answer to that question is "Everyone and everything." In principle, nothing can be excluded. We cannot embrace the whole world at any moment, but we still have to be open to learning from any source that might present itself.[17]

These three tasks—*presence, receptivity, and responsi-bility*—are actually not a sequence of steps in 1, 2, 3 order. Rather, they are a rhythmic pattern, where each task arises out of the prior one, is related to it, and incorporates it as part of itself. Presence exists within receptivity and response; response and receptivity include each other as well as presence. This is also true for *inclusion, leadership,* and *outreach.* These three are in a necessary relation to one another. When we begin to realize this, we see that each task contributes to the educational work of our fashioning as a people. For each is a curricular task, not in the sense of book-learned activity, but in the sense that it arises out of the entire course of life itself, and specifically out of the environment constituting the curriculum of community.

In chapter 1, I noted the tension of the local and the global influencing church education today and will return to it more directly in chapters 7 and 8. But here it is crucial to point out that although these six central curricular tasks are most often learned in the parish and the family, they do not stop there. They cannot stop there; if they did, they would call into question the entire curriculum of community and convict it of insularity and isolation. Instead, when genuine, these six tasks possess an inner dynamism that makes them transferable and translatable beyond the places where we originally learn them. For although originated for us in local church and family, they are able to bring us, even as we bring them, into all the other communities of our lives. These are the ones we know well, such as our job or a class in school or a bowling team to which we belong. But even more important, tasks such as these six fuel the movement that must be ours today. This is the fashioning of an ultimate curriculum of koinonia—the creation of a world community of communities which incarnates our best dreams and possibilities. It is the governing, convicting reality of a global community still unrealized, where death shall be no more, neither shall there be mourning nor crying nor pain; a community where God wipes away every human tear, and where all things are made new.

REFLECTION AND PRACTICE

Exercise 1: Questions for Musing and for Discussion

This exercise can be prepared for at home or done alone; it can also be done as a group.

1. What are at least three circumstances that led to your belonging to the church where you are now a member?

2. Would you classify yourself as a traditional church person for whom the church is essential, an involved person for whom it is central, a contemporary person for whom it is special or privileged, an independent person for whom it is valuable, or in some other way? Why do you see yourself as one or the other of these?

3. In what ways do you see the relation of the other members of your group to the church? Do you agree with their self-assessment?

4. In what ways is community a *governing* reality in your church?

5. In what ways is community a *convicting* reality in your church?

6. In what ways is community a *still-unrealized* reality in your church?

Exercise 2: Redesigning Your Congregation

In this chapter, we have spoken about different forms of church life that are emerging in the church today.

Imagine that you (or your group) have been asked by the congregation and the pastor to devise three plans for redesigning the church in its forms of church life, so that it is more attentive to the needs of all members, especially those who are alienated.

1. What forms are you going to propose: Smaller groups? Larger groups? Lay-led groups?

2. How will you go about implementing them?

3. What steps can you take immediately?

Exercise 3: Inclusion and Alienation: A Questionnaire*

The following characteristics have been found to be reasons for attraction to particular parishes. When parish members are asked to rank the items from 1 to 10, with 1 as most important, the results can give an overview of what is important in your particular community.

- The opportunities to participate in community service
- Living in the neighborhood
- Friends and/or relatives belong to this church
- The quality of friendliness and/or concern among members
- The quality of the preaching
- The prestige or status of the church in the local community
- The opportunities for leadership by the laity
- The quality of pastoral care and concern provided by the church staff
- The style of worship in the church
- The attention given to children by the church

*Adapted from Notre Dame Study.

Exercise 4: Inclusion, Leadership, and Outreach

These three qualities were named in this chapter as central to the educating power of the community. As a group, you are to brainstorm five practices that can be conducted under each heading and then choose to implement one in the next month. The other four can be chosen as agenda items in subsequent monthly meetings.

Inclusion:

Leadership:

Outreach:

Exercise 5: Dramatizing Family Qualities

The following activity is adaptable to many situations—a whole church meeting, a parents meeting, or a retreat for parents and children. Its purpose is to see how different family members see presence, receptivity, or responsibility in the family setting.

First, be sure everyone understands the meaning of the three qualities. Then choose one of the following to be demonstrated to the whole group. You will be given forty minutes to create, imagine, or act a situation (either in mime or with dialogue) that represents one of the following:

- An incident where parents or a parent is present to a child or a teenager
- An incident where parents or a parent is not present to a child or a teenager
- An incident where a stranger comes to, or is in, your home and the family expresses receptivity to that person
- An incident where a family member (an adult or a young person) tries to describe a calling that he or she has but where other family members try to tell the person that he or she is wrong
- A moral situation where a family member demonstrates responsibility to another family member but refuses to take responsibility for the person, allowing the person to come to his or her own taking of responsibility
- A situation of moral conflict where a family member

—either a parent or a child—is torn by conflicting loyalties and where other family members help the person sort out the conflict

Be sure to debrief each situation, taking time to explore how different persons felt in dramatizing the situations.

Notice if there are any different attitudes or approaches on the basis of age.

Draw conclusions for family life as a whole.

Exercise 6: Family of Origin and Family of Choice

This exercise is especially helpful in situations of marriage preparation and pastoral care. It is for two persons planning to live together. They are to write a series of letters, describing in detail their families of origin, with reference to such details as expressing affection, holidays, parental relations, prayer, etc. Then they are to compare and contrast these with their future hopes for the family of choice they are beginning together.

5

Leiturgia:
The Curriculum
of Prayer

In the course of time, every community normally establishes patterns and rhythms in its ways of being together. In families, for example, meals and chores, traveling and leisure time take on characteristic forms. Indeed, one of the great discoveries of childhood and adolescence is our sudden notice of the various ways families other than our own do things—from eating the big meal at midday to kissing or not kissing every family member good night. At work too, assignments and expectations, initiatives and proposals are carried out according to more or less set procedures developed over time; and in moving to new jobs, we necessarily have to do both unlearning and re-learning of these patterns. If we are students in school, we discover our own rituals, such as sitting in the same places in classrooms, as well as our own creating of regular patterns for taking notes, raising questions, and writing term papers.

When a community is a Christian community, one of the central patterns and rhythms it develops is a communal life of prayer, a characteristic set of forms for addressing the mystery of God. It is the community's prayer life we examine in this chapter, through the particular lens of prayer as a form of curriculum. Although prayer is often taught specifically as part of the curriculum of schooling, our focus here is prayer as a component of the curriculum of educational ministry. We are educated *to* prayer, and we are educated *by* prayer. And that education can happen anywhere and everywhere, not only in classrooms. It can happen in church and at home certainly, but also on a bus, at a ball game, on the job, while going for a walk, or while visiting in a nursing home, holding the hands of someone we love.

This second great form of religious life, received from the tradition, is leiturgia: the church living out its pastoral vocation to worship and to pray. The English word "liturgy," often translated as "the work of the people," comes from the Greek word for public service. Because of this meaning, the word "liturgy" has come to be associated with the church worshiping as a body, together as a people, and less so with the personal prayer life of church members. Although I want to highlight the communal, corporate meaning of leiturgia in this chapter, I also wish to examine more personal forms of prayer that also contribute to the life of the whole body of Christ. As John Westerhoff has noted, liturgy best refers to "the activities of a people . . . that include both cultic life (ritual celebration) and daily life."[1]

Forms of Prayer in the Church

Basically, prayer means request, petition, or entreaty, but often, especially in the presence of the Divinity, it expands to include praise, thanksgiving, and expressing sorrow over our failures and the evil in our lives. One of the best-known teaching devices for introducing others to prayer is the acronym ACTS: adoration, contrition (or sorrow), thanksgiving, supplication. Generally and appropriately, prayer is offered to God, to the One we address reverently as Father, Mother, Spirit, Holy One, or simply "Thou." I say *generally* prayer is offered to God, since in many traditions prayer is also offered to others in the communion of saints: "Peter and Paul and all ye holy apostles, pray for us. . . . Holy Mary, Mother of God, pray for us sinners." There is also the tradition of praying to the nonhuman creation, as in the psalms where we ask the sun and the moon to bless the Lord. And North American natives are known to pray in such words as these offered to the grass: "Let me so walk upon you as I pass by that you will not be crushed by my feet. Instead, let me walk upon you in such a way that you will know, after I have gone, that I am your sister."

Some of us use many words in prayer; others need only a few words. For example, some of us use a repetition: "Thou . . . Thou . . . Thou . . . ," acknowledging ourselves in the presence of the Other, whom we wish to address and ask for favor or to whom we wish to offer reverence, praise, and thanksgiving. Others of us pray best by using set formulas, often learned through our traditions: "The Lord is my shepherd . . ."; "Our Father, who art in heaven"; "Praise God, from whom all blessings flow." Or we are helped by prayer books[2] and poetry ranging from the psalms of the Hebrew scriptures to the verses of modern poets such as Edna St. Vincent Millay, Anne Sexton, or Gerard Manley Hopkins.

Others of us, desiring imagery for God that is more extensive and more inclusive, are creating new—or recovering more ancient—formulas: toward God our Mother; to God as Music; to God as the Great Sphere, whose center is everywhere and whose circumference is nowhere; to the Bakerwoman God who knows the homely symbols of kneading, warmth, and food as revealing holiness.[3] For still others, prayer is only prayer when it is spontaneous, and many persons grow up quite at ease praying with whatever words come to mind. All these activities of prayer fall generally into two major categories: personal prayer and community prayer.

Personal Prayer

We are educated by the time we spend alone in the company of the Divine. Among the forms for doing this are verbal prayer, meditative prayer, and contemplative prayer. In verbal prayer, such as that described above, we use words to address God. In meditative prayer, we place ourselves quietly in the presence of God, breathe deeply and regularly, and think, reflect, or meditate on a particular theme, asking especially what God might wish for us in relation to this theme; how we might be present to it, receive it, or respond to it. This can be an *issue* of concern in our own life (a child's illness, a coming divorce, celebrating a promotion); it can be a *theme* that threads its way recurrently through our life (creativity, loneliness, sobriety); it can be—as it is for many who meditate regularly—a *verse* or a *passage* from the Gospels.

In contemplative prayer, we move away from these more conscious, reflective, mental powers and from specific thought. We remain in silence, attempting to listen, to wait, and to be attentive. We quiet ourselves—often through the practice of centering, perhaps repeating a mantra, a sound, or a word. ("Come, Holy Spirit," or "You alone are my strength," or "Yes," or "Om.") Or we attend to our breathing. The story is told of a wise Indian guru who when approached for counsel on how to pray responded, "Concentrate on your breathing. The air you breathe is God: breathe in; breathe out; for it is God you are inhaling." The petitioner tried this, concentrating on his breathing, and found he had discovered the secret of a profound prayer life which lasted for a lifetime. The secret: prayer is as simple and as natural as breathing.[4]

Often, we will find ourselves in conversations about prayer where someone tries to convince us that verbal, meditative, or contemplative prayer is not necessary—that everything we do is, or can be, a prayer. Perhaps this is true for some. But for centuries, most religions, including Christianity, have taught that it is necessary on occasion to go apart and rest awhile. The ancient command of Sabbath *is* a command that arises out of the human necessity and demand for rest, for doing nothing, for cessation of activity, for—as the Babylonians phrased it—"quieting the heart." This is the counsel I would advocate here. For without much difficulty, for at least a few moments each day, we can incorporate

- a quiet environment,
- a relaxed attitude,
- a comfortable physical position (not lying down, since it can make us sleepy), and
- an object to dwell upon (a lighted candle; a bowl of water; a basket of flowers; a special word, our breath),

and in the bringing together of these four, we can create an opportunity for prayer. When that becomes habitual, we will find that we are crossing over into a country of the spirit where we are bringing, not prayer, but a prayerful attitude to everything we do.[5] To some degree, we are not doing prayer so much as becoming prayer, in the same way that T. S. Eliot speaks of our being in touch with music at such depth that we are the music, while the music lasts.[6] We may also find that such practice is enabling us to live more or less consciously and, increasingly, in the presence of God.

Corporate Prayer

Our prayer lives are only half grown and half developed if our prayer is exclusively personal. To complete our education in prayer, we need not only to know of forms beyond the personal, we need to experience them by engaging in prayer with others. *The curriculum is in the praying.* As with personal prayer, there are several forms of corporate prayer, but the central element is that corporate prayer is, by definition, prayer where the agent is not us individually but us as a praying community. On one hand, this is a support personally in the dry times when we experience no relation with God at all—times when we must depend on the strength and fidelity of our companions to buoy us up and strengthen us. It is even a support in the green times, where we need the discipline of a group commitment. But most of all, corporate prayer is the form we need to create and re-create our identity as a people, for leiturgia is at root "the people at prayer."

One familiar form of corporate prayer is the *prayer*

group. Many local churches and parishes have prayer groups that meet either at the church or in the homes of group members. One of the members can serve as group leader for a stated time (a month or a year) in order to get things going; or the leader/facilitator can rotate with each weekly meeting. Many find that a fine time for such meetings is early morning: the Catholic daily Mass, the prayer breakfast for people going to business, or the weekly youth group prayer meeting before school. The format can vary. It can be a set, fixed procedure where the group agrees to meditate on scripture each time and then to reflect on the meaning of that scripture for personal and public life. It can be a recitation time: for saying psalms, singing songs, or offering petitions. It can be a time of exploration where a range of prayer possibilities follow one another week by week: a Quaker meeting, a dialogue prayer, the rosary, or community stations of the cross where the group walk together to places in the neighborhood where today Jesus falls for the first time, Jesus meets the women of Jerusalem, Jesus is nailed to the cross, or Jesus is buried. Prayer groups are invaluable smaller communities of prayer when the entire church community comes together to worship: a leaven in the whole. We being many are one bread. And all of these forms of corporate prayer, in which such groups take part, educate to the pastoral vocation.

A second form of corporate prayer, more common in Catholicism than in Protestantism, yet increasingly important in both traditions, is the *retreat.* Sometimes "retreat" actually translates as "weekend workshop" and is filled with activities of entertainment, leisure, and community. These will probably not be entirely absent from a prayer retreat, but the form I am describing here is the retreat where either for a full day, for overnight, or even for a weekend or longer a community of any size goes apart from its regular setting even if it is to someone's home, takes all the phones off all the hooks, and concentrates on the one thing necessary.

Retreats can be especially helpful for homogeneous groups or for groups wanting to address a single subject with a degree of depth and in a sustained manner. Michael Warren, who has done considerable work with young people, has written recently that "in this country, youth retreats have never been used so widely or so well as they currently are."[7] This is also true for women examining our religious lives together. Retreats are also a critical source of education in prayer for boards of deacons, parish councils, church staff, Sunday school faculty members, or divorced men and women. They also are a continuing resource for families in their many alternative forms, including mother-daughter retreats and father-son retreats. The important point to make regarding curriculum, however, is that a retreat, as a form, is not a kind of disguised schooling, where lectures are given about prayer and where people take notes. The curriculum of a retreat is that a group of people come together to pray— and to be educated *to* prayer, *by* prayer, and *in* prayer.[8]

The central and essential corporate prayer is, ideally, the service of worship in which the entire community takes part. I use the term "ideally," because, it must be said, at this time in Christian history the service of worship for more than half of church people is not the central and essential rite it was meant to be. Less than 50 percent of church members regularly participate in church services in this country. Why is this so?

In *Living the Faith Community*, John Westerhoff ventures five explanations.[9] (1) *Psychosocial pathologies.* People either produce a pathological split between the sacred and the secular or use ritual and liturgy for escape and God as a kind of magic. This is a coercive, manipulative attitude where a people engages in liturgy in order to *use* it. (2) *Conflicting rituals, worldviews, and value systems.* People are exposed to so many rituals—political, economic, civic, school, entertainment, and television rituals —that a relativism develops which drastically limits the influence of any one ritual, such as weekly worship, and tends to weaken its impact. (3) *Cultural pluralism and cultic inadequacies.* We are such a diverse and varied people that our particularities (age, race, ethnicity, gen-dcr) are lost or not attended to in ritual, whereas the universal vision often presented has no resonance in our daily, ordinary lives. (4) *Cultic shallowness.* Our worship is marked by an absence of imaginative or artistic vision and by either a misuse or a nonuse of symbolism, the nonrational, and the playful. In their place is a highly stylized, rational, and above all *talky* ritual which leaves no room for persons to encounter God through their artistic, aesthetic sensibilities. (5) *Cultic ineffectiveness.* The worship service fails because it bears no fruit in the lives of the participants. Either it keeps them morally unchanged and shores up their worst prejudices or it suggests that the point of worship is that people are present to have a good feeling. (Or, in contrast, they have come in order to be reinforced in feelings of inadequacy, often being scolded by the preacher.) What it does not do is challenge or confront, along lines suggested by Annie Dillard, who writes: "Ushers should issue life preservers and signal flares; they should lash us to our pews. For the sleeping god may wake some day and take offense, or the waking God may draw us out to where we can never return."[10]

Because of these and other factors, reforms have been taking place for some time in public liturgy. Where reforms have been successful or, even better, not needed in the first place, we discover that the worship is almost always characterized by the opposites of the five inadequacies just named. These are the worship services that *do* integrate sacred and secular, or refuse to allow that distinction, claiming that all reality is sacred; *do* acknowledge differences in worldviews; *do* anguish over the dimension of depth in worship and the power of the symbolic imagination; *do* challenge all present to their own best possibilities; *do* affirm the attempts of people to live religiously and morally in the midst of life. More simply put, these are the worship services that concentrate on the proclamation of the gospel in its priestly, prophetic, and political demands, and on the human longing to *be:* in adoration and wonder and love and hope in the presence of God.

Although much still remains to be done, many churches are beginning to do the serious educational work of reshaping this particular ecclesial form, leiturgia, with end (the search for meaning and purpose) and without end (the awareness that the worship of God is never-ending). These refashionings and reshapings are the curricular tasks and educational components of leiturgia.

Curricular Tasks

In order to educate through personal and corporate prayer, at least four tasks are critical in the contemporary church. First, a church must attend to spirituality through the work of pastors, staff, and congregation to the same degree it attends to teaching, preaching, and finances. Second, it must refuse to divorce prayer and action for justice. Third, it must design services of worship that foster multiple roles and multiple involvement. And fourth, it must be a center for resources.

Spirituality

One of the dominant religious phenomena of our time is the rekindling of interest in spirituality. The hunger for deeper, more profound life on the part of church members is expressed variously: from inappropriate acting out sexually in a search for love, to the often-posed question, "Is this all there is?" to the frenzied accumulation of material wealth and the desire for more. In the face of the pain that such activity often masks, as well as in the face of direct reports and acknowledgment that the search is for a spirituality, the community needs forms in response.

Here is where the interplay of kerygma, diakonia, didache, koinonia, and leiturgia is markedly manifest. For spirituality grows in a church community through *all* of these, and the major work here becomes the recognition that whatever form of educational ministry we engage in *can* help foster spirituality. Prayer is, as we have seen, central to the enterprise, and generally the starting point, which is why spirituality is addressed in this chapter. But spirituality is more than prayer: it is, at root, *our way of being in the world before God.* In other words, nothing in our lives need be beyond the reach—the touch—of our spirituality; wherever we are and whatever we do can be bathed in the mystery of God.

In fact, each of the forms of educational ministry is also a form of spirituality: there can be a spirituality of parenting (the way some of us *be* in the world before God), of teaching, of service to others, of prophetic speech, or of quiet contemplative stillness. Pastors and teachers can point this out, but it is the vocation of all the members of the church to discover their own spiritualities, affirm the spirituality of one another, and deepen the practices that enrich everyone in the community.

Integrating Prayer and Justice

As with spirituality, the damage done by separating the forms of ministry from one another is evident when we examine how often prayer has been privatized. Nowhere is this more evident than when the curriculum of prayer is taught as quite different from the curriculum of action for justice—especially the actions of kerygma and diakonia. The task this sets for a community probing its pastoral vocation is the search to integrate—to bring together —these two great aspects of the single vocation to be the body of the Christ in the world.

Three ways to foster this search are to draw on scripture, to examine our tithing or financial practices, and to hold an annual justice retreat. Drawing on scripture in both personal and corporate prayer—perhaps by using the church bulletin and certainly by using the sermon—we can focus regularly on the biblical injunction to justice. We can pray Isa. 58:6–7—God asking, "Is not this the fast that I choose: . . . to share your bread with the hungry, and bring the homeless poor into your house, . . . and not to hide yourself from your own flesh?" We can pray Micah 6:8 (acting justly, loving mercy, and walking with God as

essentially related). We can pray the great last judgment
scene of Matthew 25—"As you did it to one of the least of
these . . ."

In addition, we can suggest that for a month or even a
year, the focus in our prayer groups and our worship
should be the question of where—as a church community
—our practices of tithing and our assignment of revenues
reflect our prayer life and our refusal to separate prayer
from issues of justice. When a church does this, it often
results in a decision to send as much as a third of church
income to a poor community in its own neighborhood or
to an adopted congregation beyond our national borders.

But because such decisions need time and space for
reflection and care-full thought, the retreat is an ideal
setting to do such probing. This is particularly true if the
group on retreat is a powerful one: the board of deacons,
the parish council, or the faculty of the church school. If
a corporate plan for the wedding of prayer and justice can
be designed out of the prayerful circumstances and prepared environment of a retreat, the life of the church as
a justly prayerful community can be faced and eventually
embodied.

Multiple Roles and Involvement in Worship

It must be admitted that worship in many circumstances can be described as Westerhoff describes it above,
since it is static, dead, and the "same old thing." One of the
reasons this is too often so is that the same person (unfortunately, often the senior pastor) does the same thing for
years without incorporating the suggestions of parishioners or allowing for alternative approaches. Actually, the
problem is not the form—which is often preset by the
church and/or the denomination and in harmony with the
tradition—as much as it is how the form is incarnated and
enfleshed.

To speak of multiple roles in worship is to speak of including as many persons as possible in the actual worship
service: from children praying the opening prayers to

dancers or dramatists enacting the sermon to situating baptism and confirmation and the anointing of the sick in the midst of the worship—and also, as is often done, the marriage ceremony—so that the participants in those ceremonies are included in worship roles.

Such participation usually arises out of involvement at many other times and places of preparation. Many churches will have one Sunday a year on which the youth group is responsible for the readings, prayers, and so on, and spends considerable time getting ready. The practice I am advocating builds on this. What I propose is a liturgy committee (with two- or three-year terms for members to ensure rotating membership and new ideas, but also with invitations to belong issued directly by the pastor), a committee involved *every single week* to assist in preparations. Two of the most fruitful examples of this kind of involvement I know are the church that invited twelve family units a year and the church that invited fifty-two. In those settings, a different group was responsible each month, and in the second case each week. Personal bonding and ownership of the liturgy was one result. But the new life infused into the worship service was the greater gift—not only because of the originality and care offered but also because the suggestions came from people living in a rich variety of circumstances. This is one of the finest ways to overcome cultic ineffectiveness, cultic poverty, and liturgical lassitude.

A Center for Resources

The growing interest in prayer and spirituality has brought forth a plethora of resources that need to be made available to church members. (Many are listed in the notes for this chapter.) From displays in the vestibule and during the coffee hour, to a church library that focuses on prayer, spirituality, and justice, to the visits on a regular basis of different leaders of prayer, to listing in the church bulletin persons who are, or would be willing to be, facilitators of prayer groups, the local community can foster the curriculum of prayer by seeing itself as providing all of these resources—and others. Indeed, some parishes take this set of activities so seriously they now have on staff a minister of prayer. In some cases this person is ordained, but in others it is a member of the community who has lived into this vocation by doing what the curriculum of prayer ought to do for everyone: educate people to pray regularly in such a way that they have become contemplative, reflective suppliants before God at some times, holy doers of justice at others, and worshiping members of a worshiping community always.

REFLECTION AND PRACTICE

Exercise 1: Questions for Musing and for Discussion

This set of questions can be used for the church membership as a whole, to get some sense of the community's attitudes toward prayer. It also may be used for a committee charged with responsibility for the curriculum of leiturgia.

1. Do you pray regularly?

2. Is your prayer more a prayer of adoration, of sorrow, of thanksgiving, or of request, or is it more generally a combination of these?

3. Do you talk about your own spirituality? How?

4. Is spirituality something different from justice, in your view, or do the two presuppose each other?

5. What is the most important aspect of worship in your church?

6. What aspect of worship is most in need of change in your church?

7. Would you, or your family, be willing to assist in the preparation of liturgy one Sunday out of the year?

8. Would you be willing to be leader for a prayer group on a rotating basis?

9. How have others in the parish, including the pastor and staff, been resources to you in your prayer life?

10. How have you been a resource to others in the parish, including the pastor and staff, in their lives of prayer?

Exercise 2: Integrating Prayer and Justice

Following are the fourteen traditional stations of the cross, with the fifteenth, the resurrection. You may do several things with this exercise: (1) Reflect on where these stations have occurred in your own personal life; (2) reflect on where, in your local community and neighborhood, these stations are going on today; or (3) plan beforehand, as a group, a walk in your area (often at a time such as Good Friday or in commemoration of Yom HaShoah) to acknowledge those contemporary stations where once again Jesus falls, is crucified, and rises.

1. Jesus is condemned to death.

2. Jesus is made to bear the cross.

3. Jesus falls the first time.

4. Jesus meets his mother.

5. Simon of Cyrene helps Jesus carry his cross.

6. Veronica wipes the face of Jesus.

7. Jesus falls the second time.

8. Jesus speaks to the women of Jerusalem.

9. Jesus falls the third time.

10. Jesus is stripped of his garments.

11. Jesus is nailed to the cross.

12. Jesus dies on the cross.

13. Jesus is taken down from the cross.

14. Jesus is laid in the tomb.

15. Jesus, the Christ, rises from the dead.

Exercise 3: Designing Liturgical Rituals

The following are ways to design rituals the entire church is planning to celebrate or remember together, or to assist in reflecting on these rituals. They are particularly appropriate for groups that come together regularly to pray or to probe their spirituality as a community.

1. Plan the baptismal ceremony for your first child, including:

- Naming
- Godparents—why are they chosen?
- Who should be present in/at the ceremony
- A short homily, describing your wishes for the child
- A short invitation to the whole church, explaining what you wish from them as community members

2. Plan an initiating ceremony for one who wishes to become a member of the parish community. Decide on:

- The meaning of membership to be communicated
- The verbal elements in the ceremony
- The nonverbal elements (music, gesture, graphic or pictorial art, symbols)
- The nature of ritual activity to be included, such as standing, coming forth, laying on of hands
- The assurances the community will make to the person
- The assurances the person will be asked to make to the community

3. Plan the ritual/ceremony for your own funeral. Choose:

- Time of day
- Kind of service

- Symbols you wish to represent you and your life
- What kind of music should be played, if any
- What kinds of comments (eulogy) should be made, if any
- Words of blessing or interment to use at the end of the ceremony

6

Didache:
The Curriculum
of Teaching

*What &
now is taught*

The Greek word *didachē* ("a teaching"), which comes
from *didaskein* ("to teach"), is a word with a hallowed
history in the Christian church. Repeatedly, Jesus was
teaching *(ēn didaskein),* in the synagogues and in the
Temple, especially on the Sabbath. People knew him as
teacher and "addressed him . . . as *rhabbi, didaskalē,* and
epistata."[1] From as early as the time of Eusebius of Caes-
area, it was known that a treatise called *The Didache* existed which was so important that in some churches it was
considered on a par with the apostolic writings that came
to form the New Testament. The ordinary translation of
the title was "The Teaching of the Apostles." But even
before that, the first Pentecost signified a time when
teaching and instruction were essential: "And they devoted themselves to the apostles' teaching" (Acts 2:42).

This in turn was an activity related to the Hebrew counsel in Deut. 6:6–7 and to the centrality of teaching and
study in Jewish practice then and now: "And these words
which I command you this day shall be upon your heart;
and you shall teach them diligently to your children, and
shall talk of them when you sit in your house, and when
you walk by the way, and when you lie down, and when
you rise." Didache was a form of Torah: direction, instruction, information, guidance on the road.[2] Because of asso-
ciations such as these, and the broad range of meanings it

110

can encompass, I use "didache" in this chapter as the overall term to designate the curriculum of *teaching*. I also use it to include those activities associated with the curriculum of schooling, which is fundamentally a curriculum giving place to verbal instruction, literacy, and study.

The existence of a set of teachings, as well as the existence of the vocation to teach, helps us get at a twofold partnership in the curriculum of teaching. First, there is a body of knowledge and behaviors that is taught; second, there is a set of processes through which this body is communicated—processes that *as processes* are teachings in themselves. Both are essential; both form the curriculum. Without realizing it, we often concentrate only or centrally on the first—the doctrine, message, or verbal understandings that form the lore and the laws. These become the exclusive curriculum. But curriculum must include the second as well: it must also be seen as equivalent to the actions, processes, and procedures through which *the* didache is taught. It is this twofold meaning of didache that concerns us in this chapter.

In terms of *what is taught,* the history of the church focuses on one central point: the incarnation, life, passion, death, and resurrection of Jesus of Nazareth, who has become the Christ. Our formulas for baptism continue to recognize this, where the candidate for baptism is asked to respond to the questions posed by the Creed: "Do you believe in God, the creator of heaven and earth?" "Do you believe in Jesus, his only Son, who was born, suffered, died and is risen?" "Do you believe in the Spirit of this God, in the church which is the people of Jesus, in the forgiveness of sin, and in the resurrection of your own body?" "Do you believe that he will come again, to judge the living and the dead?" The manifestation of God in the Christ is at the center of Christian belief and teaching, and when we remember this central belief, and mediate it to one another through teaching, ours is a priestly act.

But teaching, and the Creed, are also prophetic. For teaching is not only toward knowing and understanding the Christ of the Gospels, toward making this lore a part

of us, it is also toward examining the implications the lore
has for our own lives. It is about how we act as well as about
what we think. It is toward asking and responding to the
question, "What would you have me to do?" It is toward
a willingness to hear and live the answer (which we have
already seen in the curriculum of leiturgia): "To do justice,
and to love kindness, and to walk humbly with your God."
It is toward learning our vocation "to loose the bonds of
wickedness, . . . to let the oppressed go free, . . . to share
your bread with the hungry, and bring the homeless poor
into your house. . . . Then shall your light break forth like
the dawn" (Isa. 58:6–8).

And teaching is political. It is toward the building up of
the body politic of the Christ by continually striving to
make that body be, in form and in polity, the kind of
organism where power is never power over or power
against, but power used *with* and *in favor of* and *for* one
another and the wider society. Teaching is toward creating the situation of koinonia where all may be one; an
activity of mutuality and helping others claim their own
best possibilities, not only for themselves but for the sake
of the Christ and of the world God loves. Understood this
way, the political dimension of teaching impels toward
learning in the context of the entire planet and therefore
coming to know other peoples' religious interpretations of
God and the world as well as our own.

But to get at these meanings, and to explore what they
mean for us in our lives and in our world, we need to make
use of certain *processes* through which the didache is conveyed. These form the second aspect of the curriculum of
teaching and take a number of different forms. To begin,
there are processes that are internal to the church—intra-
mural forms such as catechesis and preaching. But there
are also understandings that are sometimes less developed, although they are part of the heritage of teaching
within the church. These processes have received particular attention in the modern world. They are those understandings emphasizing questioning, analysis, and liberation, to which today's churches are returning with fervor.[3]

Each of these forms of didache must be considered essential in the forming and re-forming of curriculum.

Forms of Didache

Internal Forms

Catechesis. The New Testament does not use the noun "catechesis"; instead, only the verbal form "catechize" *(katēcheō)* is found, with its meaning of "to hand on what has been received." In fact, the New Testament is itself a catechesis, and the specifically Christian teaching it contains is designated by a variety of words: way, doctrine, tradition, word. The catechesis takes different forms. Hebrews 6:1 distinguishes elementary teaching from that reserved for the proficient and gives the content of the first instruction about the Christ: conversion, faith, resurrection, eternal sanctions, baptism. In contrast, Luke 24:47 speaks of preaching repentance and forgiveness to all nations in the name of Jesus.

In time, catechesis becomes especially associated with the catechumen—the candidate for baptism—and as the catechumenate develops, the word takes on more specific meanings: there is baptismal catechesis, prior to the sacrament; and mystagogical catechesis, subsequent to it, the latter term revived recently through the reintroduction of the Rite of Christian Initiation of Adults (RCIA), which is also a form of leiturgia.[4] Three characteristics eventually became fixed: catechesis was doctrinal, centered on the Creed; it was moral, centered on the behaviors implied by the teaching; and it was set in the context of the liturgical, worship life of the church—not in classrooms. However, as the catechumenate disappeared and children began to be the chief focus of instruction, the term "catechesis" disappeared too.

In the sixteenth century, beginning with Luther, catechesis was revived as the need for basic instruction in the faith became more apparent and more urgent. (This

continued association of the term "catechesis" with basic
instruction is one reason I take the term "didache" as
more inclusive and more extensive.) The shape it took
with the Reformers, however, and then later with the
Counter-Reformation of the Catholics, was the "catechism." Although the intention in creating them was an
understanding of the living word of God, and the books
proved to be an essential compendium of references, the
catechisms eventually became institutions in themselves.
Their texts—rather than what and the One to whom the
texts pointed—became the focus, and the need for reima-
gining the nature of teaching in the church became obvious.

Our own time has seen a renewal of emphasis on
catechesis in the sense of traditioning faith to new members, with slightly less emphasis on its other sense of being
coextensive with the teaching of the faith, from the first
announcement of the kerygma to the developed forms of
theology. The centrality of scripture and Bible study has
been incorporated to an extraordinary degree. And although the term itself tends to be used more by the liturgical churches, the meaning of catechesis as instruction in
the faith is seen as a fundamental task of didache throughout all Christian churches.

Preaching. The other form of didache essential to as
well as internal in the church is preaching. In much of
modern society, to preach to or at someone is considered
a negative activity. Although it must be admitted in
honesty that this attitude has infected the church, preaching continues to be central, not only as a core element in
worship but as the major opportunity most practicing
Christians have for elaborating on and elucidating the
texts of the scriptures. Preaching is the form through
which and by which the church takes time to reflect as a
community on the word of God spoken in its midst as well
as on the meaning that word has for daily life. When it is
what it should be, preaching is not "random notes on religion and life" or, worse, the cult of an individual or "the

religious self-expression of the individual."[5] Instead, it is the apostolic proclamation and interpretation of the gospel.

It should be noted here that preaching is also and even more centrally a form of kerygma—of proclamation and prophetic speech—than it is of didache. Preaching is distinct from the act of teaching although not separable from it. I shall return to this distinction in the next chapter, especially the characteristics of preaching as oral, communal, and prophetic. However, I name the issue here because one of the unfortunate consequences of separating the different aspects of ministry from one another—which I am challenging in this book—is illustrated precisely in this matter: preaching has not always been understood as having a *didactic* as well as a *kerygmatic* aspect. In addition, it has communal, liturgical, and outreach aspects too. When these interconnections go unrecognized, congregations have difficulty assuming that their ministry as a whole—including preaching—is educational. Indeed, this may be one of the key reasons why many of us tend to relegate "education" and "teaching" to the church school.

When we examine preaching as a form of didache, however, we recognize how rich a component it may be in the church's coming to understand and know its own life, and in the refashioning demand accompanying that life. "What is at issue in preaching?" Karl Barth asked, responding, "Decisively that the community, and with it the world, should remind itself or be reminded explicitly of the witness with which it is charged; that it should find reassurance as to its content; that reflected in it Jesus Christ Himself should speak afresh to it; [and] that it should be summoned afresh to His service in the world."[6] Preaching at its best is a form of explication and analysis, of application to personal and community life, and of assisting Christian people to reappropriate the demands of baptism. For some, it is not only the main way, it is the only way, they are instructed in their own fashioning as a people.

Contemporary Forms

In addition to the catechizing and proclaiming aspects of didache alive in the church's work, contemporary understandings of teaching, stressed in our modern world, also have an impact on the church's educational life. Teaching is not only initiation into the church's life, and handing on the tradition; it is not only the application and explication of the scriptures. Teaching is also the act of reinterpreting, questioning, analyzing, and even at times rejecting and resisting. Such activity is of course in the treasury of the church's history, especially in the Hebrew prophets and in the life of Jesus of Nazareth, although I think it fair to say that as a set of processes such activity has not always been given pride of place. But in an era of worldwide communication and of universal questioning, it has become critical once again. Teaching includes naming those places where the tradition is found wanting and where even the Bible must be called into account—not only with adults but also in teaching the youngest Christians, so they will not have to unlearn at some later date.[7] Teaching religiously today also includes the study of religions and religious insights other than those in our own tradition, oftentimes those which conflict with it, challenge it, or call it to account.

In this view, teaching becomes the work of raising questions. It is the work of saying to learners, "Accept no dogma without investigation, it might be wrong," as well as saying, "Reject no dogma without investigation, it might be right." Teaching is the work of instructing others to ask, "Why is this so?" "Who says so?" "On what grounds?" "Are there other equally valuable perspectives on this issue?" "Have we included the testimony of the losers in this controversy or at this church council as well as the winners?" "Have we new light on this text that changes its meaning?" Teaching means assisting others to take seriously Rainer Maria Rilke's counsel to

> be patient towards all that is unsolved in your heart and try
> to love the questions themselves like locked rooms. . . . Do

not now seek the answers; that cannot be given you because you would not be able to live them. And the point is, to live everything. Live the questions now. Perhaps you will then gradually, without noticing it, live along some distant day into the answer.[8]

Once again, the person who has assisted us to do this in our own time is the Brazilian Paulo Freire. Freire is the philosopher of education who points out to us the nonneutrality of pedagogy, the idea that everything that is taught and learned carries a particular perspective with it. He is also the one who has taught us to reject the "banking theory": the image of teaching in which knowledge is "deposited" into a learner's mind, to remain there untouched and unexamined until an occasion such as an exam or a test requires the person to write a "check," calling up those deposited funds and returning them intact to the depositor.[9]

A broader understanding of teaching, therefore, highlights the power within catechizing and preaching to raise questions and where necessary revise interpretations in a wider context than present practice often admits. One way this occurs is through realizing that whether in church or beyond, teaching is itself a fundamentally religious activity in the sense that it is always, at root, in the direction of deepest meaning, ultimate origin, and final destiny. Often, if we become sensitive listeners, we find that the tradition itself is asking the questions, and the questioning is not only by us but of us and our situations.

A Meaning for Teaching. This is why, perhaps, if teachers in the church would take off their shoes on each teaching occasion in the conviction they are on holy ground, they could envision this truth more easily. They could come to see that teaching is the incarnation of subject matter through various ways of fashioning, forming, and embodying subject matter, which leads to the revelation of subject matter—the moments of "Ah!" and "Aha!" and "I see!" And at the heart of the revelation teachers and

students together could find that the deepest revelation is
of their own vocations to be subjects of existence before
God—subjects who together live out the pastoral vocation
to fashion a people, a church, and a world.[10]

Curricular Tasks

Given the pastoral and educational vocations described
in chapters 1 and 2, and the meaning of curriculum as the
course of the church's life, the tasks most closely demanded in the curriculum of teaching are not difficult to
discern. I have alluded to them in passing, but here let me
name them directly: (1) the need to underscore the wide
range of settings in which teaching occurs; (2) the need to
develop a repertoire of teaching forms; and (3) the need
to approach a broad range of topics under the rubric of
"subject matter." The first two are related to didache/
teaching in its process aspect; the third is related to it in
terms of content.

A Wide Range of Settings

An unnecessary limitation placed on teaching in our
contemporary world is the relegation of teaching to only
one of its forms: *school* teaching. For some, teaching is
assumed to be an activity that goes on only—or predomi-
nantly—in schools, and thus the enormous number of
places where human beings teach one another tend to be
overlooked, or at best classified as informal.[11] To its great
credit, the Christian church at its best has never operated
from this point of view in actual practice. Catechesis and
preaching, to take our first two forms, are understood to
occur more appropriately during worship or in the context
of liturgy than in classroom settings; community and family, as we saw in chapter 4, are natural teaching situations,
although the setting for such teaching is only rarely in
classrooms.

Church members need to be alerted to their pastoral
vocation to teach, therefore, in all the places they live: on

the job, with their children and with their parents, in situations of advocacy where speaking (or not speaking) in the face of injustice teaches others, in activities of service and outreach where what we do instructs so loudly that people do not notice what we are saying. In most circumstances we are asking of one another, "Where does your life teach me about my life?" Thus no one place is *the* teaching place, for every place can be the setting for others coming to know, if not explicitly, then certainly implicitly.

In some denominations and churches, the ordination service includes words to the newly ordained that name that person's taking on the role of pastor *and teacher.* To universalize this vocation, we need to create rituals in which we set apart all in the church as participants in the vocation to teach. Certainly this includes those in the church school. Certainly it includes parents. But to remind everyone of the other less obvious experiences of teaching in their lives, congregational ceremonies can be a help. We can engage in these at worship, either through proclamation, scripture readings, special laying on of hands, or by the choice of teaching as a special theme. We can do it by listing all in the church as teachers in the church bulletin. And we can do it by reinforcing the more specific roles of teaching in the church school program, so that many more are included than instructors, even as those specifically commissioned to instruct are assisted and affirmed. Persons can participate in teaching as aides, as support staff, as committee members, as guest lecturers, as guest preachers, and as one-on-one counselors, guides, and classroom assistants.

A Repertoire of Forms

Even as the wider vocation of all in the church is affirmed, we must continue to strengthen and support those in the specific, although more limited, role of "school-teacher"—or catechist or instructor—because they are so often our delegates in traditioning the lore and the laws. An essential practice for doing this is to offer to such teachers—through workshops and ongoing formation on a regular basis—opportunities to develop a repertoire of teaching forms, a wide range of possibilities whereby they may convey subject matter to those they are teaching. The learning in such ongoing formation could then be shared with the wider community.

The extraordinary differences in persons' modes and ways of learning demand this repertoire: some of us are auditory, others tactile, some imaginative or physical in our appropriating new material. Some of us come to know best through active experimentation, while the rest of us are more comfortable with concrete experiences, reflective observation, or abstract conceptualizing.[12] Recent research suggests that women often differ in their characteristic modes of knowing from men.[13] In addition, the "stuff" we are teaching lends itself to different ways of being conveyed. Catechesis is doctrinal and moral and liturgical. Not everything is learned best by talking about it: think of great music, great art, prayer, or action for justice.

Luckily, in church circles, we are inheritors of a wide variety of teaching forms. Norma Everist, for example, elaborates on eight of these ways: presentation, worship, discussion, inductive study, individualized learning, confrontation and clarification, experimential learning, and journal keeping.[14] Margo Strom and Bill Parsons teach engagement with the terrible history of holocaust and genocide by giving us detailed, explicit processes to complicate thinking.[15] Thomas Groome has given us the form of shared praxis.[16] Don and Patricia Griggs have produced excellent guidebooks on everything from storytelling to celebrating Advent to praying the scriptures to the art of teaching.[17] And in my own work, I have elaborated on verbal forms, earth forms, embodied forms, and forms for discovery.[18] I have pointed to the verbal forms we use, besides discourse, such as:

poetry	parable
psalm	drama
satire	mock courtroom

questions   case studies
choral speaking   songs;

the earth forms which teach, such as earth, fire, water, air, and sacrament in such activities as:

lighting candles	burning petitions
lighting fires for warmth	using breathing exercises in prayer
tending lawns for the old	washing babies
molding clay	simulating baptisms
growing a garden	observing a cocoon become a butterfly;

the embodied forms which teach whether these are our personal embodiment or our church communities—Christ's body—doing such things as:

filmmaking	videotaping
kite flying	silk-screening
portrait painting	dancing
museum field trips	taking nature walks
potluck suppers	putting on a play;

and forms for discovery, such as spending three days in a strange city with a dollar in your pocket; giving flowers to strangers; putting on the mask of a clown and walking silently through a shopping mall smiling at people; trading workplaces with someone in your congregation for a day; pretending for a few hours—with others in the church—that you are someone born in the first century.[19] Such are the forms in which insight is unveiled and genuine revelation or discovery occurs through the activities demanded in the form itself.

From a broader perspective, the point I am trying to make in naming these forms is the central point of this book. Teaching occurs through a wide range of forms. The individual teaches, the community teaches, and the offices we hold—as pastor, director of religious education, director of music—teach. But beyond that, the great forms of ministry teach: koinonia, leiturgia, didache, kerygma, and diakonia. Priestly ministry teaches; prophetic ministry teaches; and political ministry teaches. So does the absence of any or all of these—teaching's null curriculum. Most teaching is verbal, but it is certainly not exclusively so. To come to the realization of this truth is to discover the wealth of resources surrounding us and to realize we are blessed with innumerable ways to fulfill the command of Jesus, "Go and teach."

Going Beyond the Tradition

Ironically, one of the most powerful ways to sustain the tradition is to study and to face subject matter that is at first glance not related to it or that is even apparently removed and at some distance from it. This century has found religious and Christian educators enlarging the scope of the content of the curriculum by beginning the movement in this direction, notably by incorporating the insights of developmentalists such as Lawrence Kohlberg, James Fowler, Carol Gilligan, Jean Piaget, and Erik Erikson, which has brought psychology in as subject matter; the wisdom of sociologists such as Rosabeth Kanter and Robert Bellah, which has enriched the church's understanding of social form; and the vision of scientists such as Pierre Teilhard de Chardin, Fritjof Capra, and Lewis Thomas, who have taught us the intimate relation between modern science and the mystical life.

But we are still lagging behind in the Christian practice of didache in the question of how we incorporate religious insights other than our own—ones drawn from Sufism, Buddhism, Islam, and, above all, contemporary Judaism, or even from Christian traditions that are African, Asian, or Latin American. Other religions are still sometimes seen as adversaries rather than as companions in the search for wisdom. With Judaism, especially, too much teaching still conveys the notion that this religious people have been superseded and are no longer needed. This is a vision which not only is patently untrue but also ignores the fissure of evil crossing our century, the Holocaust of

European Jews. In this instance it is important to take account of the Christian teaching of contempt,[20] no matter how difficult, as a way of realizing that responsibility is sometimes evaded through the failure to remember, acknowledge, and mourn.

Finally, with reference to Christianity, we still operate from a largely European and North American bias, only very recently seeing the potential for wisdom found in cultural traditions other than our own—the Asian contemplative gift, the passion of Latin America, and the power of community which fuels the African understanding. Even within U.S. borders, we are yet to place black, Hispanic, North American native, and feminist visions at the center; we are yet to be redeemed and liberated by their transforming power.

Yet these are the incorporations to which didache challenges: to the curricular task of making companions of all those views which are at present peripheral or unattended. Only in doing this work, and placing it at the heart of curriculum, can we truly become a whole church educating a whole church to engage in ministry in the midst of the world.

REFLECTION AND PRACTICE

Exercise 1: Questions for Musing and for Discussion

1. Which three persons were outstanding teachers in your life before you were fifteen? (They need not have been schoolteachers, although schoolteachers are not excluded.)

2. Which three persons have been outstanding teachers in your life as an adult?

3. What leads you to remember them as outstanding?

4. Do you see any of their qualities in yourself as teacher?

After reflection, share your responses with one, two, or three other persons.

Exercise 2: Ourselves as Teachers

In a group, reflect on the past week, and select three times when you taught another person. Be specific about the incident or occasion:

- Where were you when the teaching occurred?
- What caused you to teach?
- What were you trying to teach?
- What did those you were teaching learn?
- What did you learn about yourself as a teacher from this experience?

Exercise 3: Coming to Religious Faith

Draw a time line of your life from birth to the present. Along this line, mark moments of religious learning, religious insight, or deepened religious understanding.

Signify who or what precipitated your learning, who or what "taught" you. Was it a person, a place, a thing, an experience, or other?

Share your responses with one or two other persons and see whether you can draw any conclusions about teaching.

Note how many people refer especially to the experience of teaching in the context of the church.

Exercise 4: A Conversation with Your Own Teaching

In the keeping of journals, a common exercise is to have conversation with our work, our future, our past, or our bodies. This exercise draws on that practice. You are asked to write at least three pages of dialogue—conversation— with your own teaching, to personify the teaching you do in your life and, by this dramatic form, to discover what it has to "teach" you. A sample beginning might be:

SELF: I need to greet you as we begin this conversation and to say hello.

TEACHING: Thank you. I look forward to this, since we do not often speak with each other.

SELF: That is true, but I am trying to find out when and where I teach and how I seem to go about it.

TEACHING: Well, where would you like to start?

Exercise 5: Reflectors for Teachers in the Church School Setting

In observing schoolteachers and/or catechists and sharing observations with them, or in jointly observing teaching via videotape, you might raise the following questions to assist investigation and understanding:

1. How would you describe the teacher's use of gestures and of other vehicles besides language: facial expression, posture, etc.?

2. Is there any appeal to personal experience on the part of either teacher or student? If so, what do you make of it?

3. Does the teacher's face reveal any nonverbal clues? What about the faces of the students? Can you draw any conclusions from observing them?

4. Are you able to pick up the mood of the teacher and students? If so, how would you describe it?

5. What is the physical situation of teacher and students? How do they sit (or stand)? What does this say?

6. Who is doing most of the talking? What might this mean?

7. Are any student-to-student interactions observable? What are they like?

8. What do you notice about student interactions with the teacher? What are they like?

9. Are all the people in the situation using language the same way? Is the teacher using technical language? Jargon?

10. What do you have to say about power in this setting? Is it power over, power against, power with, power for? What might this mean?

7

Kerygma:
The Curriculum
of Proclamation

Among the treasures of grace in the Christian tradition, none are more hallowed than the grace and gift of kerygma. Based on the Greek notion of the act of proclamation *(kēryssein)*, entrusted to a herald *(kēryx)*, kerygma has always been taken to mean both what is proclaimed and the act of proclaiming.[1] For Christians, the proclamation is the life, death, and resurrection of Jesus, the Christ; of a saving God whose word is with and for the people being fashioned. The entire kerygma has also been noted as "a remarkable departure from the ordinary approach to reality and from the traditions of classical philosophy."[2] For the writers of the New Testament were filled with two essential convictions: God had become human in Jesus, and, as incarnate, Jesus was the Primary Word. But God was also enfleshed in the words and message which were information, announcement, address, summons, and proclamation about this remarkable Presence in the world. The Divinity itself was *in* the word. The challenge of the Hebrew prophets and of Jesus of Nazareth was not only that they spoke *of* God's name or *in* God's name, or *about* God's doings. It was greater than that. Their belief was that it was *God who was speaking in their words.*[3] The Word had become flesh; the Word would go on being flesh throughout the centuries. And the implication for our own times? Today the word is becoming flesh in us.

Meanings of Kerygma

To speak of the curriculum of kerygma, then, is to speak of a complex, multilayered, richly textured reality. It is to speak of the word as that *by* which we are educated and *to* which we are educated. It is to speak, as C. H. Dodd did, of "the most comprehensive term available for the whole range of that which it is the business of the Christian ministry to convey to the faithful and to the world in general so far as it will hear."[4] It is to come to know ourselves as personal participants in that word: as *subjects* who speak it, as *mediators* who reveal it, and as *listeners* who hear it, in the image of God who is also Subject, Mediator, and Listener. Even more, in the ongoing fashioning of ourselves as a people, it is knowing ourselves revealed as a *community* that is a *subject* too, corporately speaking this word; as a gathered people embodying and *mediating* the word by the forms of our life together; and as a bonded group of *hearers,* attending to what is being said to us as God continues to speak in the creation surrounding us and to listen graciously as we attempt to respond.

This is not to say there is not also a specific meaning to kerygma. Certainly it is a long-held belief that the original kerygma—as message—may be identified with the preaching of the apostles in Acts 2–13 and with Paul in 1 Cor. 1:23 and 15:3ff.: the preaching of the passion, death, and resurrection of the Christ. That is the original scriptural kerygma in the Christian church. But what must be understood about that original kerygma is its active, alive, and powerful force over time and throughout time; its renewing and renewable rootage in the church and in each Christian; and its spatial, local, and temporal character. What must be understood, especially in an educating church, is its meaning now and for the future—its being as a word not only of the first century but of the twentieth, not only of Nazareth but of Nebraska and Nairobi. What must be understood is the life sedimented within it which moves us to reshape it with end and without end.

Such meaning and reshaping are nourished and illuminated by scripture, church, and theology. In the Hebrew Bible, proclaiming the word of God was the charism of the prophet, as instructing was of the priest and counseling was of the wise man or woman.[5] *Dabar* ("the word") came to the prophet as a dynamic entity with its own distinct reality, just as it comes today. But it was never thought of as a sound alone. Rather, it was real, almost tangible, though invisible presence. *Dabar* was often parallel with *ruach* ("breath, spirit"); once spoken, it remained in existence, carrying on its activity indefinitely. It had an objective reality; it was something concrete; it was endowed with the power of the one who had spoken it. Nowhere is this so majestically rendered as in Isa. 55:10–12:[6]

> For as the rain and the snow come down from
>   heaven,
>   and return not thither but water the earth,
> making it bring forth and sprout,
>   giving seed to the sower and bread to the eater,
> so shall my word be that goes forth from my
>   mouth;
>   it shall not return to me empty,
> but it shall accomplish that which I purpose,
>   and prosper in the thing for which I sent it.

The ecclesial and theological—and also, religiously educational—elements that stand out in this scriptural message are many. To begin with, we can be assured that the answer to the question, "Is there any word from the Lord —for me?" is a resounding "Yes!" Our living in the present is nourished by the presentness of the proclamation of a speaking God. To announce such a basic fact is also to say that even now God is present in, to, and for the world, which is to say, in, for, and to us. It is to say that the good news has arrived: God is here, God is now, God is forever with us. We can count on that. In all our struggles and pain, joys and celebrations, we are not alone. Over the

bent world, as Gerard Manley Hopkins wrote, "the Holy
Ghost broods with warm breast, and with ah! bright
wings." Over the bent world the Spirit speaks as well.

Theologically, however, we are learning the ironic truth
that the word is proclaimed with special power, and also
with special affection, to the little ones of the earth, to
(ironically) the unheralded, the unsung. We are renewing
our understanding, as a people, of Jesus' kerygma with
reference to himself and his mission, and exploring its
implications for ourselves.

> And he came to Nazareth, where he had been brought up;
> and he went to the synagogue, as his custom was, on the
> sabbath day. And he stood up to read; and there was given
> to him the book of the prophet Isaiah. He opened the book
> and found the place where it was written,
>   "The Spirit of the Lord is upon me,
>   because he has anointed me to preach good news to the
>   poor.
>   He has sent me to proclaim release to the captives
>   and recovering of sight to the blind,
>   to set at liberty those who are oppressed,
>   to proclaim the acceptable year of the Lord."
>   (Luke 4:16–19)

The poor, the captives, the blind, the oppressed: these are
our brothers and sisters. Kerygma: preaching and proclaiming their release from bondage especially where we
are the ones responsible for the bondage, through sins of
omission or not caring as well as sins of commission, such
as creating unequal economic and political structures. In
our local churches—and beyond. In our own denominations and faiths—and beyond. In our neighborhood, our
state, our country—and beyond. All peoples, everywhere.
No one is meant to be the other, the outsider, the not me,
the dispossessed. Instead, the me is you, the we is us, the
other is myself. I look in your face and I see mine—even
if you are another age, another race, another sex. The
kerygma makes that clear, demanding that we hear this
word and speak it, enflesh it and incarnate it, take it up
and live it. It demands that we do not return the word to

God empty but instead, in our lives, make it seed for the sower and bread for the eater. If we fail in doing that, our words, no matter how poetic, are false.

In essence, therefore, the kerygma is the word of justice, provoking us toward a curriculum of justice. It is an error to think of the Bible, or even of the Christian vocation, as concerned with justice as one in a series of virtues, such as peace, compassion, forgiveness, and love. Instead, the biblical kerygma is the clue we have that the entire word is a word of justice, that any word spoken by God is the word of a God of justice, and that justice is the ground of being. A richer, more complete meaning of justice shines in the Bible, shadowing the narrower legal, juridical, and antiseptic notion so pervasive in contemporary society. For in the Bible, justice is recognized as fidelity to the demands of all our relationships[7] and to the truth that we are related, quite simply, to everything. Justice arises out of passionate caring, out of desire to share the gifts of God's good earth with human and nonhuman,[8] so that we *can* be faithful. And the ways we have to encourage and enable such struggle and fidelity—such faith—exist in the church's heritage, as food for the journey and bread for the wilderness. These are the great verbal forms of scripture, theology, and preaching, the bases for the curriculum of proclamation.

Forms of Kerygma

Scripture

In one sense, the entire book you are reading now is about the Bible. Yet in underscoring scripture here, explicitly, I am pointing to its primary role as the essential documentation preserving the original kerygma, and as such, giving us nothing less than our identity as a people. The scriptures are our "personal papers": the evidence of our adoption, the sources revealing to us who we are. The scriptures tell us from whom and whence we have come; they give us our lineage. They teach us we were born in a garden and are destined for a holy city and that along the way are deserts and other gardens and cities and a continuing search for home. They remind us that our God is a revealing God whose own identity has still not been entirely disclosed, a God who offers us continuing revelation and the paradoxical security of living in mystery. They offer us the ongoing task of fashioning the texts themselves, including the need to reintegrate the Hebrew Bible rather than make it simply a precursor to the Christian gospel. They provide us with clues toward recognizing the face of a people fashioned by God.

Yet, as important as what we think the Bible *is,* even more important is what we think the Bible *means* and what—as God's word—it counsels us to *do.* Here the work of biblical scholars of this century has been invaluable, including those who have pointed out the places where the Bible itself fails to live up to the kerygma. Our curriculum work will certainly be curtailed if we do not depend upon these scholars. But we must depend on all of them. As Robert McAfee Brown notes, "We used to take account of how the Bible was read (by the critics) in Tübingen or Marburg. Now we must take account of how the Bible is read (by the practitioners) in Solentiname or Soweto."[9] But we must also take account of ourselves, in community, and make the choice together whether the Bible will be a comforting companion (as it well may be), domesticated and tamed so as to give us no trouble, or permitted to be what it in fact is: a challenge and a vocation, moving us through the difficult work where we "nurture, nourish and evoke a consciousness and perception alternative to the consciousness and perception of the dominant culture around us."[10] We must allow it to help us find our own voices.

Theology

Assisting us to speak from such deeper consciousness is a second form of the word—that form where we stand back in order to reflect, to conceptualize, to interpret, and to think. Theology is the intelligence at work, probing the meaning of the religious experience recorded in the Bible and in contemporary life, and at its best making the contribution that only the thoughtful mind can make. This is, of course, not everything, and we do well to be guided by the counsel of Gustavo Gutiérrez:

> All the political theologies, the theologies of hope, of revolution, and of liberation, are not worth one genuine act of solidarity with exploited social classes. They are not worth one act of faith, love and hope committed—in whatever manner—in active participation to liberate human beings from all that dehumanizes them and prevents them from living according to the will of God.[11]

Nevertheless, as Gutiérrez' work as a theologian reminds us, theology does have a role to play, especially in our own time when we no longer have theology so much as we have theologies—a series of distinct yet related perspectives on living the life of a people of God.

Such plurality is a new, or at least renewed, form of kerygma insofar as it reminds us that we bring a plurality of perspectives, life situations, ideologies, cultural circumstances, and assumptions to our understandings of kerygma—and that we need each of them. During the last two decades, white North American and Western European men, especially, have been asked the same question over and over by people who are neither white nor male nor North American nor Western European: "Why is what we do called 'liberation' theology (or 'black' theology or 'feminist' theology,' etc.) and what you do called 'theology'?" This question enables us to see that no one theology can be normative, precisely because of our human diversity. But what can be proposed and subsequently drawn upon—what can constitute the curriculum of kerygma— are the conversations that ensue when theologies engage one another and even allow themselves to be corrected and chastened by one another; when each recognizes its partners as in possession of at least a partial insight; and when those who sometimes denigrate it recognize that the capacity for reflective intelligence, for the life of the mind, and for serious intellectual search continues to be the strongest ally to concrete action that human beings have yet discovered.

Preaching

As a nonordained Catholic woman, I have not been brought up to think of myself as having access to the form of preaching as a way of being educated to and by kerygma. I can participate as a subject in scripture and in theology, but unless I am asked to be a guest in a pulpit, preaching is not a form to which I have continuing access. Or so I once thought. But two personal experiences have changed my mind and illuminated the meaning of preaching for me.

The first experience is my ongoing involvement in art and artistic process. Through the years, I have come to see that art is a speech that intends not so much to communicate as it does to express. I meet some reality, and even if no one else understands, the force of the reality draws, provokes, urges me to poetry or to song or to sculpture or to dance. Art is the vehicle I have to respond to the nonordinary, the ineffable, the lovely, the strange. Like preaching, which is itself an artistic form, art expresses rather than analyzes.[12] It proclaims, announces, and often heralds. And it is available to all of us whenever we need it.

The second experience is my more recent work in holocaust education, especially in the context of Christian education. I have discovered, in ways similar to my artistic involvement, that this event in my own history and in my own century, and in its relation to my own Christian religious tradition, is so critically important that even when my friends and my students do not wish to hear (and this is sometimes the case), the reality in itself demands speech —often in the form of proclamation, announcement, verbal notice, or preaching. If I do not speak, the stones will cry out.

The relation these have with preaching as a form of the curriculum of kerygma is, I believe, apparent. For the activity of preaching—the form we have received as a people—was born out of experiences analogous to those I have described. Something happened. Something continues to happen as the Unnameable One extends invitation, life, love, and hope to humanity and to the whole creation. And the human heart and spirit are so touched by this invitation that proclamation, heralded speech, and glad tidings must be told. Yet evil is also present, in the tissues of daily life and in the horrors of corporate tragedy and world disaster. Fissures of evil cross our own century, from the Armenian genocide to the destruction of European Jews to unremitting global hunger to the nuclear madness which threatens our existence and that of the planet. And before these we must also speak. Listen to Robert McAfee Brown:

> The roof of the crematorium at Birkenau, the deathcamp of Auschwitz. We are standing on ruins the Germans tried (unsuccessfully) to obliterate, to hide evidence that six million Jews had been shot and gassed and burned in such places, solely because they were Jews. I reflect: if Golgotha revealed the sense of God-forsakenness of one Jew, Birkenau multiplies that anguish at least three and a half million times. For the rest of my life, this crematorium will represent the most powerful case against God, the spot where one could—with justice—denounce, deny, or (worst of all) ignore God, the God who was silent.
>
> Of what use are words at such a time? So many cried out to God at this spot and were not heard. Human silence today seems the only appropriate response to divine silence yesterday.
>
> We remain silent. Our silence is deafening.
>
> And then it comes—first from the lips of one man, Elie Wiesel (standing in the camp where thirty-five years earlier his life and family and faith were destroyed), and then in a mounting chorus from others, mostly Jews, the great affirmation: *Shema Yisroel, Adonai Elohenu, Adonai echod,* Hear, O Israel, the Lord our God, the Lord is One.

At the place where the name of God could be agonizingly denied, the name of God is agonizingly affirmed—by those with most reason to deny. I shake in the tension between my impulse to deny and their decision to affirm.

Because of having stood *at Birkenau,* it is now impossible for me to affirm God in the ways I did before.

Because of having stood at Birkenau *with them,* it is now possible for me to affirm God in ways I never did before.[13]

And so, preaching: the form most obviously dwelt in by the pastor on Sunday, by the homilist in a liturgical setting, but in no way limited to that situation. Preaching: a word that in daily speech may have gotten a bad name, especially when it is assumed to be equal to lecturing. Preaching: an oral word, meant to be heard and received; a communal word, done because of a community or on behalf of a community or in the midst of a community. And finally, a prophetic word, a word spoken with the same original conviction that moved the Hebrew prophets. Before some realities, especially those of great joy and great sorrow, the Divine Joy and the Divine Pity must be expressed. At times, God sings in the prophet's words; at other times, God rages. But at all times, the community must take responsibility for creating an environment where that Voice may be heard.

Curricular Tasks

This brings us, most specifically, to the activities demanded of a community that would include kerygma as a constitutive element in curriculum. What are the precise tasks, educational in nature, asked of a community that has received the proclamation of the gospel? Because kerygma is word/speech/voice, and because kerygma, like all the elements of ministry, is priestly, prophetic, and political, the answers are near at hand. The activities are threefold: priestly listening, prophetic speech, and political advocacy. Each is a focus on word.

Priestly Listening

If the word continues to be sent forth to water and nourish the earth, we need, as a fashioned people, to cultivate the receptivity and responsiveness that characterize genuine listening. Whereas the curriculum of community helps us deepen our awareness of all who speak God's word to us; whereas the curriculum of prayer hones this capacity and readies us for the words that address us everywhere; and whereas the curriculum of teaching instructs and interprets meanings that address us, the curriculum of kerygma focuses on the actual listening itself: the education that comes in the listening. The specific, original kerygma of Paul and Acts, while being itself, is also a symbol, reminding us that we are being spoken to continually. A special word set apart in a single moment, it educates us to what words might be in every moment. The words of scripture, theology, and preaching point to all the other words constantly addressing us: those of earth, water, fire, and air; of animal and plant life; and most of all of other human beings. Fifteen minutes of silent listening each morning can attune us to the voice of creation throughout the day and be a reminder that the human action of speech is always partner to the human action of still, quiet listening.[14]

Prophetic Speech

The curricula of community, prayer, and teaching are incomplete without kerygma. For at some point the words heard, learned, and spoken must be placed in alignment with the prophetic role inherent in kerygma. If the priestly word is "Yes," or "Speak, O God, for I your servant hear you," the prophetic word is "No. I must refuse to let false words pass. Now is the time for my human voice— and our community's voice, as a people—to be raised against injustice."

Three educational principles can empower us in taking

on this task. The first is a suggestion from John Fry, who writes:

> I propose that theologians write theology from the stand-point of the mother in Bombay (or Pittsburgh) whose child has just starved to death. She would not be theology's primary reader, and her situation would not provide theology's subject matter. [But] her rage and grief would provide its angle of vision.[15]

In our local churches, we might not—with Fry's theologians—always be speaking about such mothers and children. But the point is that in whatever speaking we do do, whether at deacons' meetings or in Sunday school preparations or at reviews of budgets or on simple social occasions, the words we do speak must make sense, must not be obscene, in a world of dying children.

At the same time, we must be guided by a second principle. This is that whenever we do know of injustice, we covenant with one another as a local community that we shall speak. We agree to burn into our bylaws that the pulpit and the sanctuary and the parish hall will be places for the word "No" to be spoken—whether that "No" is to book burning, discrimination against AIDS patients, or anti-Semitism; to patriarchy, paternalism, or sexism; or to all the small, subtle viruses of prejudice that constantly infect the body politic of the Christ. And in these no-sayings, where conflicts arise, as they inevitably do, and conflicting points of view struggle for a hearing, the community can then rest—even when it does not want to or wishes that it did not have to—in the secure knowledge that its vocation is toward discovering truth and then speaking it, and that this has been agreed to as an operating principle.

A third principle to help us here is one offered by John Baptist Metz, the German political theologian who grew up during the Nazi persecutions in his homeland. Metz speaks and writes of gradually becoming aware of the reality of these pervasive horrors and of this awareness leading him to the point where, as he puts it today, "I could never again do theology with my back to Ausch-witz."[16] The provocation and power this has toward pro-phetic speech is that it educates us, as communities, to formulate our own answers to the same kind of statement. Together, as a people, we must decide how we shall speak of ourselves: "We, the people of this church, cannot live out our pastoral vocations with our backs to _____." It may take us some time to come to a formulation of our own stance, but when it does come, it can ensure our being a people fashioned to utter prophetic speech.

Political Advocacy

Advocacy is a particular and peculiar form of speech, of the word. It is speech undertaken on behalf of others and/or for the cause of others.[17] It is not insignificant to men-tion here that in promising the Spirit to his followers, Jesus chose to name that Spirit as the "Advocate." *Dabar* and *ruach* are parallel; word and breath are related; the Word and the Holy Spirit are one. When I speak of political advocacy, however, another dimension is added. For here, the advocacy is in the public realm, in the area where legislation is proposed, considered, affirmed, or rejected, and then becomes or fails to become the law of the land. For a religious people who are attempting to educate and be educated to the curriculum of kerygma, and to shape and reshape its forms for our own time, speech against injustice will necessarily take as one of its curricular tasks the responsibility to speak in the public realm. More specifically, it will include the political tasks of identifying, analyzing, interpreting, and planning around issues con-cerning the community.[18]

In *Empowerment: Skills for Parish Social Action,*[19] Harry Fagan outlines and develops a number of the steps needed to engage in such action intelligently, from strate-gic planning, to recruiting, to defining a problem, to re-searching and interviewing, to choosing and testing issues. All of these are activities of speech—word—and are there-fore named here with reference to the community's role as advocate, in the image of the Spirit sent by Jesus—advocate for the poor, the homeless, the hungry, the dispossessed, the sorrowing, the lost.

In chapter 8, we will turn to more specific actions toward which such steps lead. Now, however, the concentration is on the action of speech concerning a particular issue and on becoming involved as communities in the work of speaking politically. In order not to speak mindlessly, we need the planning, researching, and analyzing. But we also need to take the more difficult steps of choosing our priorities. Undoubtedly these will be determined largely by our local situations, by the social locations of our particular church communities. The homelessness and hunger of large numbers of the populace in New York City may decide our choices if we reside there or in other large cities. Zoning laws designed to keep out people of color may be first priority in more suburban settings. The pollution of the environment may be our first concern in still others. But wherever we are, the curriculum of kerygma will never be null for those who listen and who care. It will reveal itself to those with eyes to see and ears to hear. It will remind us we are baptized and confirmed into proclamation: as speakers, mediators, and hearers of the word.

REFLECTION AND PRACTICE

Exercise 1: Questions for Musing and for Discussion

Sometimes the Bible is thought of as giving answers to our questions. In this chapter, however, and in the curriculum of kerygma, we realize that it more often gives us questions to our answers. Two passages used in this chapter do that: Isaiah 55 and Luke 4.

Move into groups of no more than four, if you are reading together in community, to respond to the following questions concerning each of the passages:

1. What does this passage tell you about the word?

2. What does this passage tell you about the kerygma?

3. What does this passage tell you about justice?

4. To whom is this passage addressed?

5. What was the situation when the passage was spoken first?

6. What contemporary parallels can you draw for your own situation?

7. Make a list of ways that you or your family might respond to this text in your ways of living.

8. Make a list of ways that your congregation might respond to this text in its life as a community.

9. Make a list of ways that you and your community, as Christian citizens, can influence the local, state, and national society in order to be true to these passages.

10. Choose one activity from these lists which you will begin this week. Be sure to note the day you are to start.

Exercise 2: The Newspaper as Kerygma

Every morning for a week, read the newspaper as if it were a source of kerygma. Note at least five passages each day that are words demanding a response from you and for the community.

Exercise 3: The Word of Repentance

To this date, the U.S. Government has never expressed sorrow officially for the suffering caused in Japan to those who were innocent victims at Hiroshima and Nagasaki.

Your work is to do research on these events and to single out a Japanese congregation in either of these cities, to whom you then address letters of repentance and regret.

Exercise 4: Researching an Issue

In this chapter, skills for parish social action were named. In order to face issues toward which the word of kerygma might be spoken, in the form of prophetic speech or political advocacy, you can use the following questions (drawn from Fagan, *Empowerment*):

Stating a Problem

- Who is doing or not doing something?
- What are they doing or not doing?
- To whom are they doing or not doing it?
- Where are they doing or not doing it?

For example, the Local Housing Authority (who) determines policy (what) for the residents of public housing (to whom) in our county (where) without their being represented (what).

Data Gathering: Questions to Ask

- What information do we need and what must we do to get it?
- Where or how do we get it?
- Who will get it and by when?
- How will it be reported back to the wider group?

Picking an Issue

- Is it immediate with a sense of urgency?
- Is it specific and concrete—related to local or actual people and policies?
- Is it winnable or is it giving witness?

Questions for the Working Group

- Will the other people in the parish or neighborhood accept this issue?
- Will this issue be dramatic enough to build the com-

munity, or is there a risk that a failure now would end things?

- What alternatives should be considered to ensure continued attention to this issue?
- Will this issue be satisfying and even fun so that everyone will learn something in the process?
- Will facing this issue lead to action?

8

Diakonia: The Curriculum of Service

Reaching out in service to others has been an aspect of the pastoral vocation from the beginning of Christianity. Learning it from his own Jewish people, Jesus modeled it consistently throughout his life, and after his resurrection the community of his followers was described in terms of it. "There was not a needy person among them, for as many as were possessors of lands or houses sold them, and brought the proceeds of what was sold and laid it at the apostles' feet; and distribution was made to each as any had need" (Acts 4:34–36). But even in the New Testament, the word for service, *diakonia*, which has also come to be translated as "ministry," is used in two ways. Sometimes the word has a general sense, referring to the entire range of the serving and ministering activities of the community. On other occasions it is particular and specific, designating activities such as serving at table, providing hospitality to guests (Matt. 8:15; Luke 4:39; 8:3), supplying the necessities of life or ministering to (Matt. 25:44; 27:55; Mark 15:41), or acting on behalf of the poor (Rom. 15:31).

In this chapter, I will focus on the second meaning, diakonia as specific and particular service and outreach to others, keeping in mind that the first, more general connotation must not be lost. Throughout, my intention will be toward remembering and reintegrating compassionate service as part of the essential curricular work of every

Christian community, while recalling at the same time the interconnectedness of all works of ministry within the pastoral vocation.

Restraining Elements

The inclusion of service and outreach as essential components of Christian curriculum presents a number of initial difficulties. Naming them, however, can help us recognize some of the built-in hindrances to a full curriculum of service. To cite a first, diakonia is so closely allied to ministry as a term that it can easily be made into an office or special work belonging to only a few—the pastor or the minister of education, certain officers such as members of a board of deacons, or a class of church people who form a specific, ecclesial group. Through no fault of such persons, the obligation of service and outreach can be forgotten or go unnoticed as the work of the entire community, because it is more apparently the work of some.

Even when the obligation is understood to be universal, it can wither and shrivel up into a cold, pitying "charity," especially if we attempt to be servants or serve too earnestly. Caryll Houselander talks somewhere of a woman who was one of those persons who "lives for others" and you could always tell the others by the hunted look on their faces.[1] Because of its close association with the term "servant," service is also approached with hesitation: ours is not a society of servants, and servant classes have almost entirely disappeared. Most people want neither to have servants nor to be servants.

Too, the word "servant" may not be strong enough to bear the rich, New Testament understandings of diakonia. The move to terms such as outreach, ministering, acting for justice, troublemaking, empowerment, and social care are all attempts to move away from the meaning of diakonia as *sub*servient, being under someone else.[2] Still, I do not believe the church is ready to do away with the word "service," especially if it is used as it is in the wider social sphere under the rubric of "public service." Understood as a work of compassionate ministry, both directly to persons and structurally toward unjust systems, it remains critical in the life of the church and a constitutive part of the gospel.

There is one further restraint on the curriculum of service. This one appears when the church finds itself unwittingly fostering guilt instead of graceful giving in trying to educate toward love and care for the needy and helpless. Those who teach in the arena of social justice regularly note that exhortations to do good, to help one's neighbor, or to go beyond oneself are often heard, fairly or unfairly —especially among the nonpoor—as judgments on the hearer's own life. Or the exhortations result in "compassion fatigue." Sometimes this is shored up by the presence of the dubious yet widely assumed ethical principle, "If it hurts, it's good." To love and care for one's neighbor too often translates as start hurting and stop loving yourself. Or, if that is impossible to manage, at least try not to love yourself too much.

Liberating Elements

Yet the biblical command remains: we must love our neighbors as we love ourselves. In this context, the church ought to celebrate the originating attitude toward service as gratitude rather than guilt. One basic impulse in the vocation to care and serve, where we cherish a fundamental option for the poor, incorporating diakonia as an essential curriculum, is that simply by being born and given life and freedom, we are receivers of gifts and grace. That impulse, however, can be twisted out of shape by individualism and consumerism. In such circumstances, we need to relearn joyful appreciation of all we have received and all we continue to receive. We are, in terms that Aquinas used, a *capax universi,*[3] a capacity for all the gifts in the universe. But we also need to relearn, where we have forgotten it, the truth that the gifts which so abound for some of us are not shared equally. Reaching out in service is our attempt to redress that imbalance as a work of joy, delight, appreciation—and justice: fidelity to the demands of the vocation to be brothers and sisters to all, and engagement in the structured struggle to share the pleasures of God's good earth.

As we fashion the curriculum of service, therefore, our starting point is the power of compassion. This power is the peculiar one stressed in the New Testament, especially in the person of Jesus, whose strength was manifested in a gentleness and care that saw washing feet, healing the sick, and feeding the hungry as natural and necessary. His power was a form of compassion, nurtured for centuries before him in his own Jewish tradition. Jesus was a fellow sufferer with others, aware as we must be, that it is a fundamentally religious stance to

> advocate compassion for the world's poor and suffering. Compassion, meaning "to suffer with," suggests not a pity directed at the weak but a sharing between those who *appear* to be strong and those who *appear* to be weak. The sharing of suffering reveals weakness in the strong and strength in the weak, and consequently new meanings of both "strong" and "weak." If we respond to the other as fellow sufferer, we can begin the process of channeling power in a human form. Whereas pity is the act of an individual that solidifies the inequitable distribution of power, compassion is a mutual action that protests systematic oppression.[4]

Forms of Diakonia

This power of compassion takes many forms in the local Christian community. The forms are dynamic and life-giving, and most of all liberating. They are ways we incarnate our capacity for the universe; indeed, unless we exercise them, we can become literally sick, from too much self-interest and too little reaching out. Their presence in the curriculum educates *to* ministries of service, and the persons who participate in them realize they are being educated *by* these ministries of service. The forms that lead to the fullness of diakonia are social care, social ritual, social empowerment, and social legislation.

Social Care

Care is a component of the religious and moral life that has received considerable attention recently. Both Nel Noddings in *Caring*[5] and Carol Gilligan in *In a Different Voice*[6] initially studied care from women's perspective. In doing so, they illuminated its centrality in the work of compassionate service not just for women but for men and children, even for nonhuman animals. Care is a virtue, strength, and power that involves us physically as well as mentally. As compassionate service must, the exercise of care involves the one who is caring as well as the one who is cared for. It is neither a universal, abstract concept nor a principle on which to base action. Instead, it is a way of being and doing where we are necessarily involved as we tend for one another. Care makes us receivers as well as givers: the one who is caring is always a part of, and within, the caring activity. Thus it is essentially social.

The place in the church where care has been stressed most recently is in the focus on pastoral care, especially in the training of clergy. Clinical pastoral education (CPE) programs are now required in many seminaries. However, they need to be viewed with a critical eye, especially when not extended beyond individual mental health to the whole of society. One critic articulates this concern in the following commentary:

> The pastoral care movement has been eminently successful in recruiting pastors out of the church, and out of pastoral care, into clinical care. It has been less successful but still influential in diverting pastors from the acquisition and practice of pastoral skills to clinical skills while remaining within the pastoral context. The movement has failed to facilitate and enlarge the roles and functions of pastoral care. . . . We have tended to look upon the church and the clergy as the handmaidens of the mental health movement

per se, and thereby fail to look at the particular and special contributions of the church and clergy in the overall context of the society.[7]

The author goes on to suggest that pastoral care must concentrate on the church itself as a social system which responds to human needs through intervening to change the pressures upon people. The point is that to be genuine, pastoral care must be extended to institutions (including the church as institution), provoking them to action where that is needed, calling them to account when they are sinful, and celebrating them when they enrich the human. Pastoral care needs also to be social care; if it is not the second, it may not qualify as the first.

I use the term "social care," then, to emphasize the way all acts of caring, even for ourselves, have an impact on the wider society. Care is rooted in attitudes of relation, receptivity, and response (of which I spoke in considering both the curriculum of community and the curriculum of prayer), and these attitudes contribute positively to the social order and the social fabric. We can exercise care toward ourselves, in the quiet of our own family; we can exercise it in our neighborhood and our state; and we can exercise it on a global level. We can exercise it toward people, and we can exercise it toward institutions. Most pertinently here, we can exercise it in our local parish.

Social care takes shape in familiar ways: feeding the hungry, giving drink to the thirsty, sheltering the homeless, clothing the naked, ministering to those who are ill, sick, or dying. At its best, and when this is possible, it is toward helping others to help themselves. It surfaces as an incarnating of the Beatitudes: practicing poverty of spirit, mourning with those who grieve, choosing to be peacemakers, being merciful. A Bronx grandmother, living in poverty, and raising two grandchildren with AIDS after her own daughter's AIDS-related death, recently reflected how it might work in the lives of any of us. Asked about her attitude to the father of the children, a drug user now dying of AIDS, she responded, "I used to say I would seek revenge for what he did to my daughter. But . . . if he comes home [to die] I will care for him."

Social Ritual

Besides the direct kind of ministering manifested in social care, we fashion diakonia when as groups and communities we come together in organized ways to insist on services that are missing (such as wheelchair access to public buildings, including places of worship); to pray for the presence of care (holding a prayer vigil, for example, to petition for fair housing); or to protest actions inimical or hostile to the care demanded by the gospel (the battering of women, the death penalty, the invasion of sovereign nations). Social rituals are organized actions characterized by regular, patterned, artistic movement involving groups of people banded together in reaching out. Ceremonies, vigils, marches, and parades are all social rituals. By standing silently outside weapons factories or on the border of small countries that the United States may have bullied or by taking on the identity of a sanctuary church, we participate in social rituals that both serve and reach out.

Some social rituals are quite simple and are accessible to anyone. At a school where I once taught, any of us who wished could meet weekly on Tuesdays at 5 P.M. outside the library and pray with lighted candles in hand for the coming of peace in Central America and South Africa. Other rituals are massively complex, involving national and global connections. The past decade has seen such rituals in Live-Aid, Farm-Aid, and Band-Aid, which involved millions in a corporate ritual of diakonia. Earlier decades witnessed the social rituals of freedom marches and sit-ins, and most people would acknowledge the enormous power such rituals had in creating change in social systems and social circumstances. Both the end of the Vietnam War and the civil rights legislation of the 1960s came in large part from the social rituals of speaking out, sitting in, and walking/running for peace.

Communities remembering and reintegrating diakonia

form social rituals today along similar lines. In many places, for example, annual walks for hunger draw attention to that evil in our midst. Rituals may be designed in such a way that the evil is ameliorated as well. Ladling soup or washing dishes at a soup kitchen in regular patterned ways can do this. Groups of teenagers rocking in rocking chairs, for the homeless, can too. So can supporters of gay and lesbian rights holding prayer vigils in order to influence civil or church authorities. Annual demonstrations such as the release of doves and cranes on Hiroshima Day not only reach out to the victims of the bombings, they educate toward a vision of peace. And the ritual of Yom HaShoah, the annual memorial commemoration of the Holocaust now entered in the lectionaries and calendars of many churches, not only is a way of asking forgiveness; it is a way a community can acknowledge and reject its own sins, especially those of anti-Semitism, by saying, "No. Never. Never again."[8] Local churches that have no social rituals, especially ones that reach out to the poor and hungry, need to examine their churches seriously, asking, "If not, why not?" and "If not us, now, then who? When?"

Social Empowerment

Diakonia without reflection can sometimes be limited solely to ministry *for* and *to* others: it can be direct service which, while it alleviates suffering, does not move toward enabling the suffering ones to claim their own power or does not move toward change in those social systems and social policies which perpetuate injustice. Therefore, a third and essential form of diakonia is a kind of social care and social ritual designed toward helping others help themselves and toward eliminating dependence. Dieter Hessel recounts the following story told to him by a social work coordinator in California which names some of the aspects of this form of diakonia.

> We began by giving out bags of food. Then we added an interview and referral role. But we were still creating dependence, even though many congregations supported our

direct services. The next step was to institutionalize the food pantry network with a nutritious three-day supply of food, coupled with expert help in getting emergency food stamps that very day. Then we began to ask how we could help prepare low-income people to deal with their problem more effectively. We still give out food, but we do many other things along with that.[9]

That social work coordinator had learned that diakonia goes beyond providing emergency food to helping people learn how to claim the benefits to which they are entitled. Sometimes this is done by making free newsprint publications available, as the Southern California Council of Churches did, making available its guide entitled "How to Get Food and Money: The People's Guide to Welfare and Other Services in Los Angeles County."[10] Other times this is done by *pro bono* lawyers meeting with homeless people and alerting them to their social security and Aid to Families with Dependent Children (AFDC) rights. Other times this is done by literacy programs and English as a second-language classes, in a critical wedding of the curriculum of teaching and the curriculum of service.

But the important point concerning social empowerment is that its emphasis is *not* on what the caregivers do but on conditions where the needy are able to take responsibility for themselves. Perhaps a person in a leadership role can help, but the help is toward making it possible for others to use their own strengths and powers, not the leader's. Rather than perpetuate the church's paternalism, the movement is toward relinquishing control so that others might direct their own lives.

Social Legislation

Actions of social care, ritual, and empowerment must always be twofold. First, they must be planned in a way that will address the situations of poverty, homelessness, and helplessness in our midst. Of course these are global concerns as well, but often the litmus test for our global concern is whether we are working to alleviate the suffering in our own areas, in the house next door or down the block. But second, and at the same time, diakonia must address the systems and structures that perpetuate unjust conditions. It must be a participating in the reshaping of the social order through the kind of political activity I have already alluded to as the tradition of "public service."

The suffering of people educates us to accountability. Awareness of such accountability, in turn, faces us with the need for permanent social care and permanent social healing. Structures for permanent diakonia that has end (purpose) yet is always without end (termination) are necessary because the poor we have with us always. Thus, although diakonia is prophetic in its attention to care, priestly in its impulse toward ritual, and both of these in its attention to empowerment, each of these forms is incomplete unless it is also political. Permanent social change—the redistribution of the gifts of God's good earth—does not occur by wishing it. It occurs when the imaginations of people are touched in such a way that they work to refashion existing institutions wherever those institutions prevent people from living complete human lives. ("Is not this the fast that I choose: . . . to break every yoke?" Isa. 58:6) In our societies, one way to do this is through political action, action that lobbies to enact appropriate laws and to overturn those which are unjust.

Perhaps nowhere are Christian churches more at fault than in their reluctance to engage in such action. Far too many pastors can echo the lament of one who wrote recently that, both locally and nationally, his church, especially in its boards, "will go to any extent to avoid having to become involved with the issues of the day. Hiding behind the old shibboleth, 'keep politics out of the pulpit,' the leadership of our . . . churches continues to dance around the crisis facing the church."[11] Obviously this is not the complete situation. Witness the U.S. Bishops' statements on the economy and on peace, the continuing testimony of church people before congressional committees, and the lobbying efforts of concerned religious groups. Nevertheless, just as the Synod of Rome in 595 could complain that the deacons were no longer looking after the poor but chanting psalms instead,[12] every local church in our country must be aware of the ever-present virus of inaction that blocks involvement in political life. The virus is manifest in the way monies are allocated, in the self-understanding of the nonordained that their vocation is essentially that of worshipers, and in the absence of response to legislation that pleads so fervently for our attention that the stones are crying out. We need go no farther than the minimal response to the suffering and isolation of AIDS patients and their families or lovers to see the infection at work. The virus is manifest in the negative attitudes directed toward those who do respond. Sometimes the virus is widespread; at other times it is contained. But it is there: a demon to be cast out by prayer and fasting—and by public action in spite of disapproval.

What action is demanded? Involvement in civic life. Participation in citizens' lobbies. Continuing monitoring of social legislation. Requests for reallocation of monies— always using the gospel as criterion. We do such work whenever we move to change the laws that benefit only the few. We do it whenever we plan and carry out letter writing petitions or organize political action committees (PACs). We do it mainly as a form of diakonia, but because of the interplay of curricula we also do it through all the other forms. We do it as communities who take this as a necessary element in the pastoral vocation, embodying it, for example, in organizing car pools and transportation on election days. We do it through prayer at every parish service, lifting up political legislation that faces the community. We do it through teaching, instructing, and analyzing the causes of and responses to need incumbent on the instructors and the instructed—which means that study, reading, and writing can also be profoundly caring, profoundly social, profoundly empowering, and profoundly political. We do it through the kerygmatic tasks of priestly listening, prophetic speech, and political advocacy where members of a local church seek direct contact with elected officials—and follow up their meetings by reporting back to the whole congregation, in order to decide on the response diakonia offers.

Curricular Tasks

Embodiment of the curriculum of service—personal and public—can be accomplished in many ways at the local level. But whatever way is chosen, social care, social ritual, social empowerment, and social legislation can be anchored best, I would argue, by choosing and particularizing concretely. Indeed, two essential characteristics that make a work qualify as ministry is that the work include *doing something* and that the work be done *in public*. [13] As long as a work remains completely private or at the "future topic of discussion" level, it is not yet diakonia.

That ministry of service begins with the choice to become engaged. The more particular the choice, ironically, the more universal the implications for further ministry—the suffering of one revealing the suffering of all; and the work to address one issue, and the policies surrounding it teaching attitudes and approaches applicable to others. Equally as important, choosing one issue to which attention and action will be committed is the way to move away from the limitation of inaction. And so the first task is to choose. Once choice is agreed to, education can be completed by fashioning a set of processes and procedures which address that issue.

Thus, *Curricular Task 1* is a churchwide decision to work toward redressing some social ill or need, local or global, that in one way or another touches the lives of all. A church with an aging population, or one composed of caretakers of aged parents, might well choose the care of the helpless old and the public policies that shape their lives. The presence of Downs syndrome children may spark involvement in mental retardation. An AIDS death in a community or in the family of a community member may open the entire parish to personal and public service toward this issue, especially toward affirming quality of life for AIDS patients in the face of death and demanding release of federal funds to help. Parishes with many un-documented workers or local churches close to the Mexi-can border may force the issue of sanctuary. The imprison-ment of a draft resister may call forth an effort to wage peace. Sometimes and even more simply, the impassioned concern of one member—over racism or poverty or hun-ger—may become the concern of all. Whatever issue or set of issues is chosen arises from the life and concerns of the community and is the natural follow-up, next step, and necessary partner to the work of kerygma, described in chapter 7, the work of defining, analyzing, and studying prior to choosing. *Curricular Task 2* is the actual working on this issue through all the forms of educational ministry.

In *Social Ministry,* Dieter Hessel addresses diakonia in ways that are identical to those I have argued concerning curriculum and the church. Beginning with the belief that the ministry of the church *is* social ministry and that social ministry involves all the functions of the church, he lists two modes of ministry:

First Mode	Second Mode
Liturgy (public prayer)	Social service—advocacy
Preaching	Community organization
Education fostered by the church	Public policy action
Pastoral care and pastoral counseling	Institutional governance
Empowering lay ministry	Corporate responsibility

Then he observes, "The first group of modes has seldom been perceived as social ministry; the second group has seldom been developed in regular congregational minis-try."[14]

My reason for citing Hessel here is that he begins where we are concluding, yet his position is the same: each mode of ministry forms community (koinonia), praises God (lei-turgia), teaches (didache), proclaims the word (kerygma), and affects society (diakonia). Not only are all social, all are educational. Further, these forms of pastoral and educational vocation are essentially interrelated. It is not possible to engage in one alone. For the curricular tasks of service this means that once we have chosen an issue (step one), we begin working on it (step two) through all the forms of curriculum in interplay. Diakonia—or, in Hessel's term, social ministry—is carried out by the whole community educating the whole community through each of its curricular forms.

By way of example, allow me to illustrate this with a description of work I directed with my colleague, Jane Cary Peck, and twenty-five co-ministers in a program called "Education for Social Justice Ministry." To fashion a curriculum of diakonia, we asked the participants to begin by choosing an issue on which they wished to work. We suggested racism, hunger, peace, and sexism. Then we asked them to do the following, to which they agreed to commit themselves:

1. Spend at least twenty minutes a day in prayerful meditation, either on the issue itself or on their own relation to the issue. (Leiturgia)

2. Read on the issue regularly (we provided and suggested books and articles), as well as on the nature of social ministry, in order to be informed on the issue and carry it on intelligently. (Didache)

3. Meet weekly with others from the group of twenty-five in order to bounce reactions off each other, gather support, create resources, and connect the issue with their own lives. (Koinonia)

4. Formulate their responses to these actions by reporting their experience verbally and/or in writing to the wider community: their parish, local neighborhood boards, state and federal government. (Kerygma)

5. Spend at least four to six hours *weekly* engaged in direct activity that involved them in the issue. (Diakonia)

This format, we discovered, enabled the participants to bring all the aspects of the pastoral vocation into play as they sought to embody a curriculum of service. The

prayerful, personal, and reflective component gave them
time to examine the presence of the issue in their own
lives or in relation to their lives. They could touch hunger,
for example, in contemplating their own relation to food
or to fasting. Or, as one woman who worked in a woman's
shelter did, they could take time in such prayerful periods
to mourn the suffering and abuse of innocent women and
children. The reading and study enabled their service to
be backed with data and information, especially for those
who worked in legislative, lobbying efforts. The community conversation gave them support when their own
flagged or when it seemed that no one else cared as much
as they did. The preparation of verbal reports helped
them to hone their own skills of proclamation. And all of
these actions supported the diakonia, the work itself.

That work proved to be quite varied, as it could be in
any local church. Some, working on hunger, served meals
to the elderly who depended on them daily, visiting parts
of the city they had never visited before. Others drove
mobile food vans, stopping to offer food to street people
where it was needed. Others spent their time in local,
state-operated agencies, lobbying for effective legislation
and learning many of the concrete realities of political
action. Still others, while wishing they could do the latter,
were swamped by the needs of the former. One man, for
example, although knowing the need to change legislation, and desperately eager to engage in it, could not begin
doing that because the daily demands for food and clothing in his local, urban church were so directly overwhelm-
ing he could not move away from them.

All, however, appeared to be educated to four things.
The first was that once they had seen, they could no longer
"not see." They had learned to ask the questions that
brought them to the kind of prophetic awareness described many years before by Rabbi Abraham Heschel, an
awareness moving them to become perpetual advocates,
perpetual troublemakers. "It requires much effort to learn
which questions should not be asked, and which claims
must not be entertained," Heschel had written, continuing,

> What impairs our sight are habits of seeing as well as the
> mental concomitants of seeing. Our sight is suffused with
> knowing, instead of feeling painfully the lack of knowing
> what we see. The principle to be kept in mind is to know
> what we see rather than to see what we know.[15]

This group became people who knew what they saw and learned how to respond.

Second, they realized the absolute interconnection between direct, personal service and the public service necessary toward reforming and refashioning civic, political policies. Those who answered phones in local agencies or attempted to get appointments with public officials discovered the limitations and possibilities of that work, while others found that without public help the poor continued to get poorer. Third, they learned they could not perform their service alone—it had to be in, by, and with the help of a community. And finally, as any parish group might do, they learned to birth compassion. That compassion, however, did not emerge as soft or sentimental. Instead, it was a compassion conceived in passion itself: a vehement, commanding, powerful dynamism, where, had they not cried out and acted in the face of suffering, their own lives would have shriveled and been tarnished.

Today, those of us in the church fashioning a curriculum of diakonia—of personal and public service—can do no more. Certainly we can do no less.

REFLECTION AND PRACTICE

Exercise 1: Questions for Musing and for Discussion*

1. What is a serious and pervasive condition in our society demanding social care, social ritual, social empowering, and/or social legislation?

* Questions are adapted from Hessel, *Social Ministry,* p. 191.

2. Does this condition demand Christian moral attention? If so, why? If not, why not?

3. Has this condition been neglected by people in authority? Has it been neglected by people in our congregation?

4. How urgent is attention to this condition for the poor and the vulnerable in our midst?

5. Is this condition also of interest to the middle classes? If not now, was it once of interest in the past?

6. Can this condition be addressed in ways that lead to the empowering of those affected by it?

7. Does this condition have concrete and manageable "handles"?

8. Will this condition elicit the resources of this church: talent, money, leaders' support, members' energy?

9. Are there available ways for many people to respond?

10. How can community, prayer, teaching, the word, and outreach face this condition?

Exercise 2: Photography and Social Seeing

1. Announce a photography exhibit open to all in the church with cameras.

2. Ask people with cameras to find pictures that answer these questions:

• What is oppression?
• Who is my neighbor?
• How do we reach out?

3. Arrange for a display of the pictures in a prominent place in the church community.

Exercise 3: An Inventory of Social Care*

This exercise is for any church group that meets regularly: parish council, parish leadership team, deacons, church school staff, or church school class.

1. List twenty ways this parish is practicing social care.

2. List twenty ways this parish is not practicing social care.

3. Decide, from a combination of the two lists, on five concerns that have surfaced and list these, as a group and with consensus, in priority order.

4. Find out whether any of the participants have addressed any of these concerns over the last five years at local, state, or federal levels. If they have, ask them to share the experience, describing what they learned from it and where it led them.

5. When the top five have been chosen, decide on at least three strategies for meeting these needs during the next year.

*The same exercise may be used for social ritual, social empowerment, and social legislation, although these almost always overlap to some degree.

Exercise 4: A Vocation Fair

Many churches hold a church fair as an annual event. The fair suggested in this exercise is one that offers many different ways to express the vocation of reaching out.

The vocation fair is a people's fair, with different tables or booths to represent different outreach ministries and where presentations are made in any form people choose (art, music, slides, videos, speeches, sermons, puppets, clay figures, etc.). Possible booths for the fair are:

Family booth   AA booth (also ACOA;
                                        Al-Anon)
Family Violence booth   Alateen booth
Parenting for   Odyssey House booth
   Justice booth   (drugs)
Feeding the Hungry booth   Peace booth
Hospital booth   Friendship booth
Pediatric Hospital booth   NAACP booth
Hearing Impaired booth   Central America booth
Visually Impaired booth   Sanctuary movement booth
Lazarus booth (care   Wheelchair booth
   for the dying)
AIDS booth

Exercise 5: Creating Social Rituals

This exercise shows how to demonstrate a particular issue as well as demonstrate *for* this issue. Those preparing it are asked to prepare, along the lines of sit-ins and pray-ins:

- A poem-in
- A paint-in
- A sing-in
- A play-in

Choose a particular theme as a focus, preferably a theme to which the parish is already committed to act. Divide the group taking part into four smaller groups, asking members to choose whether they wish to work on poetry, painting, music, or drama. Decide on a time when they are to report back (a week, a month).

Then, according to preference:

- Ask one group to select poems from world literature that address this issue and prepare a poetry reading
- Ask the second group to choose paintings from world art or create paintings that demonstrate the issue
- Ask the third group to choose music that addresses the issue or create songs

• Ask the fourth group to choose or to create plays that address the issue

At a specified time or on a particular date, and after report and practice, schedule the sharing of these artistic responses as a social ritual for the wider community.

PART THREE

THE
PLANNING

9

Facilitating
the Fashioning

In 1925, the great religious educator William Clayton Bower published *The Curriculum of Religious Education,* an extensive and still valuable exploration of the meaning, nature, origin, and dynamics of curriculum.[1] When Bower came to the issue of planning and designing curriculum, as we do now, he examined existing planning procedures and then held them next to the meaning of curriculum he had proposed. He did this in order to see whether meaning and planning procedures were congruent with one another—to discover whether they tallied.[2]

This is similar to the procedure I will follow in this final chapter. My basic principle in working toward design and implementation is that what you think curriculum is determines how you think curriculum is created. For example, as Bower examined curriculum resources, he concluded that the nature of the curriculum assumed was one where (1) the intention was to transmit effectively the accumulated knowledge of the past, (2) the curriculum was designed primarily for the teacher, not the learner, and (3) the processes that resulted were external to, yet authoritative for, the learner.

In the previous century, this viewpoint had governed the five steps that every schoolteacher since J. F. Herbart, their originator, learned thoroughly in normal school.[3] These were *preparation,* where the teacher starts with the student's prior knowledge (the apperceptive basis); *presentation,* where new knowledge is presented in a clear and impressive manner; *assimilation,* where the new knowledge is interrelated with the other bodies of knowledge already present in the mind; *generalization,* where the learner is led to form accurate concepts and correct definitions; and *application,* by which the newly acquired knowledge is brought to bear on new situations. Bower concluded that should the focus be shifted from materials to be taught to the person learning them, and to a meaning of curriculum as enriched and controlled experience, these traditional steps would "undergo a complete reconstruction."[4]

Having spent the previous eight chapters exploring the meaning, nature, origin, and dynamics of curriculum as it exists in today's church, we find ourselves faced with a similar situation. The Herbartian method of the nineteenth and early twentieth centuries has been complemented by a set of steps that came into prominence in the middle of the present century with the publication of Ralph Tyler's *Basic Principles of Curriculum and Instruction.*[5] These steps, the so-called Tyler rationale, have had a profound influence on educational planning, although, as with Herbart, their main referents are to teachers, students, and schools. Tyler outlined a procedure whereby designers of curriculum could analyze curricular sources (studies of society, of learners, and of subject matter), select basic objectives, generate educational experiences, and evaluate learning outcomes. Four questions directed attention to the issues entailed in curriculum planning:

1. What educational purposes should the school seek to attain?
2. What educational experiences can be provided that are likely to attain these purposes?
3. How can these educational experiences be effectively organized?
4. How can we determine whether these purposes are being attained?

Anyone who has ever attempted to design a church curriculum is likely to be familiar with these questions in some form, since Tyler's work has had a pervasive influence. Curriculum workers who succeeded him moved to an even more detailed, technical set of issues than he, ones that were overtly scientific in orientation and on occasion bordered on the mechanistic. With little variation, designing curriculum became a process where one followed a precise set of rules:

One: Discover Needs/Interests
Two: Set General Goals
Three: Define Specific Objectives (making sure they are clear, specific, realistic, and measurable)
Four: Design a Program
Five: Examine Your Resources
Six: Determine an Evaluation Procedure

Any scheme that has had such widespread acceptance is of course of value. In the case of the Tyler procedure, this has been true especially where the intentions of educational designers are to specify ways in which measurable, objective, and verifiable outcomes can be achieved. It has also been valuable in planning programs, both in and outside of schooling contexts. Yet even then, this kind of planning extends only so far.

For if we believe that education is a continuing revelation, unfolding in time many things that have not been known before; if we believe that learning has its own rhythms and cycles and repetitions; if we believe that forms and contexts themselves educate; and if we believe that, essentially, religious life is mysterious and sacred and to be faced with fundamental awe, then other forms for curriculum planning are needed. People are not infallibly adjusting organisms, able to meet predetermined objectives exactly on schedule if at all. Something or someone may break through an existing situation and transform it in quite unexpected and basically immeasurable ways. Indeed, the poor human community, made in the image of God, often does not have stated objectives. Instead, that community muddles through life, aware there will be wrong turns and missed opportunities, yet intuiting that as a community it has within itself the power to re-create and reshape the forms of its own life.

In designing curriculum, many religious and church educators have begun to question or rearrange steps such as Tyler's and Herbart's, create new ones, or, when these older ones are kept, modify them, situate them in a wider context, or make use of them as only one way to engage in curriculum planning. As we have seen, C. Ellis Nelson and John Westerhoff are among these, starting as they do with Christian community. Paulo Freire is another, working with basic assumptions such as the nonneutrality of education, the overcoming of cultures of silence, and the need to end a banking theory of education in favor of one that celebrates the human vocation to be subject, not object, of existence. Mary Boys is another.[6] In this book, we are attempting to join their company by looking at curriculum planning from a religious and artistic angle of vision, in contrast to one that is technical and mechanical.[7]

Despite such creative intentions, however, most curriculum continues to be designed from five basic assumptions that must be challenged. These assumptions are: (1) The basic curriculum work—sometimes the only work—is that of teaching, or didache; (2) curriculum is equivalent to academic resources and printed materials; (3) curriculum is coextensive with the curriculum of schooling rather than the wider curriculum of education; (4) knowing and learning and understanding are measurable, quantitative realities—products rather than processes; (5) education comes to an end and is itself some thing that human beings designated as learners go to a place to get (as in "getting an education") rather than cultivated as lifelong involvement.

To each of these assumptions, I have taken exception in this book. In doing so, I have presented an alternative vision of what curriculum is. To begin with, although it includes teaching, curriculum is not equivalent to teaching or to what can be said. It includes the *entire* course of the church's life, the play and interplay of community, prayer, service, teaching, and proclamation. In addition, curriculum—as the total life and experience of the church —can never be limited to what is printed. Printed texts are at best a valuable curriculum resource.

In summary, attention has been directed in this book to the curriculum of education, more specifically of educational ministry, and the assumptions just stated have been offered not as choices but as essential grounding for future curriculum design in the church. Anything else is simply too narrow. The pastoral and educational vocations demand that the work of church curriculum, like education itself, be never-ending.

The Church as Artist

If we would plan curriculum, then, in ways that are true to these principles, we need to think of ourselves primarily as artists and only secondarily, if at all, as technicians and programmers. This is consonant with the vision of education outlined in chapter 2, where we spoke of education as formgiving: as the re-ordering and re-creation of experience in order to give it meaning; as the continual reshaping of the forms of the church's life with end (purpose) and without end (termination); and as the commitment to more and more adequate models. Even more to the point, if our vocation is the fashioning of a people—more specifically, if our work is fashioning—we need to work as poets and sculptors and creative artists, colleagues of the brooding, hovering, indwelling Spirit. We need to take our cues from the working of imagination. We need to manifest in our work the principle that what you think curriculum is determines how you think curriculum is created. The style of planning must be congruent with the nature of what is being planned.

As in any artistic work, the originating conditions of curriculum planning are "seldom clear-cut, specific objectives; they are, rather, conceptions that are general, visions that are vague, aspirations that are fleeting. Much of

what we value, aspire to, and cherish is ineffable; even if
we wanted to, we could not adequately describe it."[8] In
addition, as we begin our planning, our goal is not to end
with the creation of materials for each of the forms of the
church's life. Instead, it is to take part in a process, where
the movement through the process takes us, in the doing,
to where we are to go.

In what follows, therefore, I propose that the planning
of curriculum follow the steps of artistic process. Like all
artistic process, such planning and designing will be a
movement through a sequence of rhythmic steps, although these steps will be akin to those in a dance—rather
than those of a staircase or ladder.[9] As such, and although
they will contribute to a whole, the steps will never come
to an end. They are guides, markers to be used as orienting
points—not rules to be followed. Sometimes they will
move us backward, sometimes forward, sometimes side-
ward, sometimes down. How long we stay at any one step
is determined by the dance itself, not by some external
clock. Generally, each step will issue out of what has gone
before, and in the execution of any step the next one will
emerge. Artists name the steps differently, and no one
naming is absolute. But because I have already explored
them at length in a previous study on religious imagination,[10] and because I am proposing that curriculum design
is a work of artistry and imagination, I will again designate
them as contemplation, engagement, formgiving, emergence, and release. A set of names such as these is itself a
factor in the creative work of fashioning a people; the
flavor and tone of these names differ from objective,
preparation, assimilation, and generalization.

Contemplation

Contemplation is the human capacity to sit back, be still,
and allow ourselves to be receptive to whatever is addressing us. Gentle, active looking and careful, active listening
are its starting points. Contemplation is a waiting upon
and an attitude of readiness to be taught, to be spoken to,

and to be surprised. It is giving ourselves enough room, enough space, and enough time to see what is really there. It is a reminder that the fashioning of curriculum needs to be done in an atmosphere of prayer and with an attitude of serenity, even in the midst of busy, complex activity.

Three fundamental issues face curriculum designers at the step of contemplation: people, present ministries, and purpose.[11]

The first issue, that of *people,* refers to our taking time to decide, in the setting of the wider church community, who will be responsible on behalf of the whole community, to facilitate the work of fashioning. Certainly the professional staff of the church will be involved, with pastor and designated education ministers taking the chief active roles. But members of all the organizations and/or committees responsible for community, teaching, prayer, proclamation, and service must be consulted and asked for delegates who will represent those essential aspects of the congregation's life. Ideally, all who participate should keep journals describing the sequence of the work and their responses to it as reports that might in turn serve others involved in similar processes.[12]

The first task will be the formation of a representative committee who will in turn be the listeners to and spokespersons for the wider community. They will be the ones who, out of their knowledge of the community's life, reshape the forms of curriculum as they take on the gritty yet exhilarating work of engagement and formgiving— steps two and three. Such leaders can be sought through announcements, through publicity in the form of folders, brochures, and posters, and through direct invitation, perhaps by using a theme such as "Behold, we are doing a new thing."

The second issue, that of *present ministries,* may prove to be more difficult. For when the representative group is formed, the task then becomes a contemplation of the entire church's life, its present ministries, and an honoring of those as its curriculum. The work includes the movement to understand that the congregation does not *have* a curriculum; the congregation *is* a curriculum. At this point no church starts from scratch, and ideally the first question is, "What are we doing now that is already forming the curriculum of education in our church?" This question will be toward identifying the already present activities—the explicit curricula of community, prayer, teaching, proclamation, and service, in the many forms each of these takes. But then the questioning needs to move on to contemplation of the implicit[13] and null curricula[14] too, to listening for those places where the actual curriculum is in conflict with the stated curriculum, and to ferreting out the unheard voices and the unused procedures. Questions that can help do this are:

> What do we hear and what do we see?
> Why do we hear and see what we do (i.e., what are our biases, prejudices, presuppositions, histories, and predilections as we contemplate and listen)?
> What don't we hear and see? What is missing? Why?[15]

The third issue to contemplate is *purpose*. Here the contemplation is of responses to such questions as where this church is going as a church. What are the hopes, dreams, and desires for life together? What is our direction? Asking these questions involves movement toward being a people aware of the pastoral vocation, toward being a whole community educating a whole community to engage in ministry in the midst of the world. To articulate our responses, we may want to draw on statements others have made as models for ourselves, such as this one which was part of the Cooperative Curriculum Project in 1965.

> That all persons be aware of God's self-disclosure and redeeming love as revealed in Jesus, and that they respond in faith and love—to the end that they may:
>
> KNOW who they are and what their situation means;
> GROW as a People of God rooted in Christian community;
> LIVE in the Spirit of God in every relation;

FULFILL their common discipleship in and to the world;
ABIDE in Christian hope. (Adapted)[16]

Others of us may want to choose a scriptural statement to
express our purpose. But in the long run, we are going to
be compelled by the gospel itself to adapt a vision for our
own community, a vision that belongs to us. For although
we are bonded to larger Christian and human community
throughout the world, the step of contemplation is only
fulfilled with the attempt to put a vision into words for *this*
church in *this* time, at *this* place, and in the lives of *this*
people.

Engagement

After taking the necessary time for contemplation, we
move to the step of engagement: diving in, wrestling with,
confronting, discovering, acting upon and acting with
what we have been contemplating. In the art of sculpting,
for example, engagement is the step where the sculptor
takes the clay into her or his hands and finds out what it
can do and what it cannot do. Hands begin to get dirty,
limits on both sides are revealed, and what is extraneous
or unnecessary is discarded. Here, eventually, is where the
work of centering can begin. Engagement is the step of
getting all our materials in order, putting them to work
and ourselves to work along with them, and getting rid of
what will no longer be useful.

When the step of engagement is brought to bear on the
fashioning of curriculum, it will have two main elements:
holding on and letting go.[17] Practically, this will mean that
the responsible committee looks at the present experience
of the people of this church in this world and holds it
against the vision statement emerging out of contemplation. With this comparing, the activity of holding on then
begins. We look at all the aspects of the church's life—its
community, prayer, teaching, proclaiming, and service—
in order to see what we must hold on to, must keep, must

continue doing in the light of the present situation and in the light of the gospel mandate and the tradition of our people. When we take the Bible, for example, we must hold our present ministry in the church against such passages as those we have highlighted as we examined each ministry, and ask:

Where are we doing justice, loving mercy, and walking with our God?

Where are we saying through our words and our actions, "Look here. This is a manifestation of this Jesus who was crucified, the One whom God has now raised up"?

Where are we continuing in the teaching of the apostles and in the breaking of bread and in the prayers?

Where are we contributing goods to each one, according to need?

But also:

Where are we failing to do so, not only by omission but by what we are continuing to do that is no longer appropriate?

What organizations in our parish do we need to let die or to acknowledge are already dead?

What people on the margins or boundaries of our parish have we failed to include or pretended were not there?

Who in the wider community have we ignored?

What demonstration of belief have we avoided because of its unsettling or troublemaking potential?

And where might any of us personally be refusing to let go of a role or a church office or a favored status, even though others in the community might exercise it better?[18]

Certainly, confronting and wrestling with such questions will not be easy and will be a place where we might draw on discernment processes or force field analysis in the course of many congregational meetings. When conflicts arise, the community will be served best by our facing them and moving them toward resolution.[19] But when we have done these things and taken the actions they demand, we should find laid out before us, as jewels on a cloth, all the facets of our church life. Or, to take an even more apt metaphor, we will have laid out, as in an artist's studio, the instruments for a new creation. We have handled them often, learning both what they can and cannot do. We know them, and ourselves, to be in the service of new life. We are co-creators, acting together. We know both where we must dig in and where we must hold back. Before us are the aspects of our life, which, if directed Godward, will make the body of the Christ a holy and vital organism, even more than it is now. Taking the aspects of that life in hand thus readies us for the step of formgiving.

Formgiving

Once, through engagement, we have set out all the facets of our congregation's life, decided what to keep and decided what to let go, we come to the central work of fashioning, the giving of form to what is there—and to what is not yet there. Here the task becomes attending to the living core of curriculum: taking in hand the five forms of the church's life and choosing to shape and reshape them in the direction of the vision we have articulated. Ideally, the fashioning committee will now move into a subcommittee phase on one hand and to an enlarging phase on the other. Some will take responsibility for giving form to the curriculum of prayer; others for that of service; others for that of teaching; others for those of proclaiming the word and of community. As they do so, they will need to reach out to include other members of the church community who are particularly gifted in one or another facet of a particular area or eager to become involved in it. This is the place where printed curricular resources play a part, and subcommittees would do well in fashioning the subject matter and processes appropriate for each curriculum to find out what is available, using it to help shape that particular ministry.

To take but one example for each ministry, the persons giving form to the curriculum of teaching may want to examine the *Kerygma* Program in order to develop or adapt the most recent material that will help in the work of schooling, with critical attention given to biblical teaching. *Kerygma* is a program that is lifelong, designed to enrich and extend existing ministries.[20] The subcommittee for the curriculum of prayer may want to take part in and adapt the Rite of Christian Initiation of Adults with its four elements of precatechesis, catechesis, illumination, and mystagogia (ongoing learning). This rite is one that educates liturgically, through ceremony and community in a setting of worship, supported by both instruction and sponsorship.[21] Or the committee might decide to initiate a series of retreats. Those giving form to the curriculum of koinonia may want to research Renew,[22] a program used throughout the world whose base is community. Or they may decide to start a house church or a youth church.[23] The group exploring the curriculum of kerygma may wish to draw on, or model, the resources of Facing History and Ourselves, a profound word of historical understanding, which relies on oral history and testimony, keeping journals, and an artistic use of videotape, literature, and film.[24] The curriculum of service subcommittee might wish to hold its own church life up against the measures suggested in Thomas Fenton's edited collection, *Education for Justice.*[25] They may decide to house a homeless family or buy a dwelling for senior citizens or proclaim the church a sanctuary parish.

Searching for and through resources, committees might also turn their attention to resources other than books: to neighborhood service agencies, national organizations, the world of nonhuman nature, the physical activities of art, sport, and play, the refreshing powers in music and song.[26] And finally, each committee would find it valuable to go through this book, read the chapter concerned with its particular ministry, engage in the accompanying exercises, and use these as catalysts for forming and re-forming that specific aspect of curriculum in the life of their own church.

The major artistry at this step of formgiving, however, will be that as they examine and study and dream and converse and re-create, people will find themselves doing exactly what is called for in the work of education. They will find they are reshaping the church's educational life with very serious purposes in mind, yet with the built-in guarantee that such reshaping will always need to be attended to as an ongoing, never-ending call. More than that, and even though it may not occur immediately or even in the first few years of conscious formgiving, they will eventually realize it is they themselves, as a people, who are the primary subjects of the work of fashioning, living stones being made into a priestly, prophetic, and political temple not built with hands (1 Peter 2:4–5).

Emergence

Attention to each of the curricula that make up the one curriculum will eventually bring the fashioners to a step where the entire curriculum is coming forth, to a moment akin to birthing. Just as a potter comes to a step where the throwing or the molding of the clay is finished, and the vessel ready for its own birth—and thus its own life—so too, a time arrives where planning comes to an end and a new phase begins. This is the phase where the potter sees that a new creation is coming into being. The moment of emergence in the church context is similar, for in fashioning the church curriculum, emergence is the step for recognizing the community's readiness to proclaim, "This is who we are" by expressing it in the presentation of "This is what we do."

To embody this, an Emergence Sunday might be proclaimed, for example, for the last Sunday in September. Alternatively, the five weeks after Labor Day could be designated, in sequence, as a time when the whole church lifts up all the facets of its life together, newly reborn, for scrutiny and heightened awareness. A three-day church fair might be held to symbolize the community's attention to this multiform life, with this church fair becoming an annual or biannual occasion. On the other hand, a church may decide to start small, beginning with a retreat for the board of deacons, or elders, or the senior adults, where the presentation of the newly fashioned curriculum occurs. Or it may choose to work with several small groups, but at different times.

For many congregations, as with formgiving, the step of emergence might not come until after two, three, or even five years of prior planning, except perhaps for pilot projects. For others, it could be an annual occurrence, a regular religious ritual at a designated time, perhaps during a festival or feast cherished in the particular community. But its characteristic feature would be as a rite of passage and coming of age, a confirming of the pastoral and educational vocations of everyone in the congregation.

Emergence would therefore necessarily be inclusive of persons as well as of programs. Just as many congregations regularly set apart occasions to honor or to present their church school teachers for community recognition and affirmation, occasions are needed for honoring and presenting the persons in the church who act as sponsors for all the other ministries. Acknowledging their sponsorship of community, service, prayer, and proclamation may be exactly the ceremonial grace needed to awaken the ministry of those who have been waiting for precisely such a call.

Whatever the process chosen, however, emergence is needed so that the church as a whole can proclaim its mission, ministry, and identity in the present and be readied for what is yet to be. It is the time to sing, "We, being many, are one body in the Christ. We understand ourselves to be a community of communities, a worshiping community, a teaching community, a proclaiming community, a community of service." When this happens, emergence functions as a sacrament of identity and responsibility celebrating this people's affirmation of who and what they are. It is a community celebration of the pastoral, educational, and artistic vocation to shape the entire course of their church's life.

Release

The final step in the creative, artistic process is letting go, releasing into the wider community the life which has been formed. Release is expressed in the routine, day-to-day living of the Christian gospel, as well as we are able, nourished and nurtured by the prior steps of contemplation, engagement, formgiving, and emergence. Release is a step especially incumbent upon the planners of curriculum who often have very precise and exact visions and who see the different paths others may begin taking with their carefully suggested and carefully thought through hopes—paths the planners may not have anticipated. Release is the step of trusting the Spirit to remain within the work as a creative presence who assists in ennobling the dance.

When a committee—even a large one with several subcommittees—has spent considerable time, energy, and psychic investment in planning, release may be a very difficult step. At some deep level, we who have begun the new thing in committee know (or think we know) best and are often hurt, challenged, or upset when the forms to which we have given birth are sent out into the broader context. We fear they will return to us empty, or worse, unrecognizable. We are often terribly afraid that we or our people will be found doing exactly those things we have sworn to avoid and have agonized over not repeating.

Nevertheless, in releasing into the community what we have created and in watching what others do with it, we are imitators of a Creator God who set out a creation of immeasurable beauty and then gave it into our frail hands. We who hope to fashion a renewed curriculum, and in doing so fashion a new people, must try to do the same. We must trust, as our God has done with us, that the dynamics of grace are there in the curriculum and in all the people, acting for and with each other. We must trust that the continuing presence of our God is a given, a promise that will not be revoked. The people receiving the curriculum, the people to whom curriculum is released, belong to God. And since God is both where they are now and where they are going, that should be enough in their lifelong fashioning as a people.

THE PRACTICE OF FASHIONING

Exercise 1: Questions for Musing and for Discussion

1. As you think about your church's curriculum as a whole, what are its strongest points?

2. What has contributed to this strength?

3. Who has contributed to this strength?

4. Where is new life beginning in the curriculum as a whole?

5. As you think about your church's curriculum as a whole, what are its weakest points?

6. What is lacking, in your view?

7. What has contributed to this lack?

8. What procedures have contributed to weakness in the curriculum?

9. Of what, in the church's life, do you need to let go?

10. If you could choose one activity as starting point to enliven or enrich your curriculum, what would it be?

Exercise 2: Preparing a Statement of Vision

In the first artistic step, contemplation, we suggested that a church take time to formulate a response to such questions as:

• Where are we going as a church?
• What is our purpose?
• What is our direction?

In this exercise, the committee on curriculum is to spend a minimum of three hours shaping its vision statement. The session ought to begin with silence, prayer, reflection, and contemplation, and with several other vision statements to be used as models, such as the one offered above, as well as pertinent scripture texts that offer perspectives on community, prayer, teaching, the word, and outreach.

Together, after prayer, study, and listening to one another in community, the committee should formulate a basic vision statement to guide it in its work—a statement to use as criterion and measure and guide.

Exercise 3: Holding On and Letting Go

The basic purpose of this exercise is to take inventory, as a committee, of the elements in the church's life that are already acting as the basic curriculum. Ideally, there should be a brainstorming of twenty elements for each of the five curricula that are to be held on to and twenty elements that may need to be discarded.

Brainstorm the twenty elements for each.

List the twenty elements for each.

Place the lists in priority order.

Having brainstormed and listed, the committee ought to come to some consensus with reference to at least three issues pro and con for each form of curriculum.

The last step is to decide on some community action that puts the consensus into practice.

Exercise 4: A Prayer for the People

Following any one of the psalms, or even some favorite hymn or prayer of the congregation, compose a prayer of emergence: an invitatory, announcing prayer to be proclaimed to the whole people when the time has come to do the "new thing."

Notes

Introduction

1. John V. Taylor, *The Go-Between God* (Philadelphia: Fortress Press, 1973), explores these two interpretations at length. See pp. 25–32.

2. Ibid., p. 27.

3. For an extended description of these forms, as well as for a rendering that applies them to youth ministry, see Maria Harris, *Portrait of Youth Ministry* (Ramsey, N.J.: Paulist Press, 1981), esp. pp. 12–26.

Chapter 1. Church: A People with a Pastoral Vocation

1. See Avery Dulles, *Models of the Church* (New York: Doubleday & Co., 1974). Dulles cites five models: institution, community, sacrament, herald, and servant.

2. In Walter M. Abbott, S.J., ed., *The Documents of Vatican II* (New York: Guild Press, 1966), ch. 1, art. 2. This quotation and others have been slightly altered to use gender-inclusive language or give more apt rendering.

3. Nathan Mitchell, *Mission and Ministry: History and Theology in the Sacrament of Order* (Wilmington, Del.: Michael Glazier, 1982).

4. In Abbott, *The Documents of Vatican II, Lumen Gentium,* par. 31.

5. It may help to be reminded here that *ekklēsia,* the term for church in the New Testament, is not so much a religious as a

civil-political concept. See Elisabeth Schüssler Fiorenza, *In Memory of Her: A Feminist Reconstruction of Christian Origins* (New York: Crossroad, 1983), p. 344.

6. In William James, *The Varieties of Religious Experience* (1902; New York: New American Library, 1958), James defines religion as the feelings, acts, and experiences of *individual men in their solitude,* so far as they apprehend themselves to stand in relation to whatever they may consider the divine. See p. 42.

7. William R. Burrows, *New Ministries: The Global Context* (Maryknoll, N.Y.: Orbis Books, 1980), p. 99.

8. Walbert Bühlmann, *The Coming of the Third Church* (Maryknoll, N.Y.: Orbis Books, 1977), pp. 20–23.

9. See Maria Harris, "Questioning Lay Ministry," in *The Laity in Ministry,* ed. George Peck and John S. Hoffman (Valley Forge, Pa.: Judson Press, 1984), pp. 33–46.

10. The first two dictionaries cited are the *Oxford Dictionary of English Etymology* and *Webster's Third New International Dictionary.* The third is Funk and Wagnalls.

11. Gabriel Fackre, "Christ's Ministry and Ours," in Peck and Hoffman, *The Laity in Ministry,* pp. 109–126.

12. See Loughlan Sofield and Carroll Juliano, *Collaborative Ministry: Skills and Guidelines* (Notre Dame, Ind.: Ave Maria Press, 1987); and James D. Whitehead and Evelyn E. Whitehead, *The Emerging Laity: Returning Leadership to the Community of Faith* (Garden City, N.Y.: Doubleday & Co., 1986).

13. For extended development of the issue of power, see Maria Harris, *Teaching and Religious Imagination* (San Francisco: Harper & Row, 1987), esp. "The Grace of Power," pp. 78–96.

Chapter 2. Church: A People with an Educational Vocation

1. See Maria Harris, *Teaching and Religious Imagination* (San Francisco: Harper & Row, 1987), pp. 34–36, 46–59, 167–172.

2. Ibid., pp. 34, 119–141.

3. Ben Shahn, *The Shape of Content* (Cambridge, Mass.: Harvard University Press, 1957).

4. The dominant understanding of education in the United States, at least in recent decades, has been that of Lawrence A. Cremin, who describes education as the deliberate, systematic, and sustained effort to transmit attitudes, values, skills, and sensibilities. See his *Public Education* (New York: Basic Books, 1976), p. 27. In my view, this emphasis on transmission and on

effort tends to neglect the wider and more extensive education which happens implicitly and without stress on either effort or human intention which is also very real.

5. John Dewey, *Democracy and Education* (1916; New York: Free Press, 1966), p. 76.

6. Gloria Durka and Joanmarie Smith, *Modeling God: Religious Education for Tomorrow* (New York: Paulist Press, 1976), p. 23.

7. Gabriel Moran, *No Ladder to the Sky* (San Francisco: Harper & Row, 1987), p. 13.

8. Gabriel Moran, *Religious Education Development: Images for the Future* (Minneapolis: Winston Press, 1983), esp. ch. 8. See also Gabriel Moran, *Interplay: A Theory of Religion and Education* (Winona, Minn.: St. Mary's Press, 1981).

9. Thomas Groome, *Christian Religious Education* (San Francisco: Harper & Row, 1980), pp. 15–17.

10. See Gabriel Moran, *Religious Body* (New York: Seabury Press, 1974), pp. 150–154, for the original use of this framework.

11. Harris, *Teaching and Religious Imagination*, pp. 78–96.

12. Adapted from Christopher Logue, *Ode to the Dodo: Poems from 1953 to 1978* (London: Jonathan Cape, 1981), p. 96.

13. See Leonard Doohan, *The Lay-Centered Church: Theology and Spirituality* (San Francisco: Harper & Row, 1984); and idem, *Laity's Mission in the Local Church: Setting a New Direction* (San Francisco: Harper & Row, 1986).

Chapter 3. Curriculum: The Course of the Church's Life

1. Howard P. Colson and Raymond M. Rigdon, *Understanding Your Church's Curriculum*, rev. ed. (Nashville: Broadman Press, 1981), p. 40.

2. *Oxford English Dictionary*.

3. Arthur J. Lewis and Alice Miel, "Key Words Relating to Curriculum and Instruction," in *Curriculum: An Introduction to the Field*, ed. James R. Gress, with the assistance of David E. Purpel (Berkeley: McCutchan Publishing Corp., 1978), p. 17.

4. Colson and Rigdon, *Understanding Your Church's Curriculum*.

5. Iris Cully, "Changing Patterns of Protestant Curriculum," in *Changing Patterns of Religious Education*, ed. Marvin Taylor (Nashville: Abingdon Press, 1984), p. 220.

6. William Pinar, "Currere: Toward Reconceptualization," in Gress, *Curriculum* p. 542.

7. D. Campbell Wyckoff, *Theory and Design of Christian Education Curriculum* (Philadelphia: Westminster Press, 1961), p. 17.

8. Gordon MacKenzie, "Curricular Change: Participants, Power and Processes," in *Innovation in Education,* ed. Matthew Miles (New York: Teachers College Press, 1964), p. 402.

9. Lewis and Miel, "Key Words," p. 21.

10. Elliot W. Eisner and Elizabeth Vallance, eds., *Conflicting Conceptions of Curriculum* (Berkeley: McCutchan Publishing Corp., 1974).

11. Iris Cully, "Changing Patterns," pp. 220–221. See also Robert W. Lynn and Elliott Wright, *The Big Little School: Two Hundred Years of the Sunday School,* 2d ed., rev. and enl. (Birmingham, Ala.: Religious Education Press, 1980), pp. 100–108.

12. Fred Newmann and Donald W. Oliver, "Education and Community," in *Religion and Public Education,* ed. Theodore Sizer (Boston: Houghton Mifflin Co., 1967), pp. 184–227. See esp. p. 219.

13. Ernest L. Boyer, *High School: A Report on Secondary Education in America* (New York: Harper & Row, 1983). It might be noted here that this suggestion has been widely and warmly embraced, especially by parochial schools under church auspices. But whether a shift has occurred in the meaning of curriculum in such schools remains to be seen.

14. *Christian Education:Shared Approaches* was approved for use in the following denominations: American Baptist Churches in the U.S.A., Christian Church (Disciples of Christ), Church of the Brethren, Cumberland Presbyterian Church, Episcopal Church, Friends General Conference, Friends United Meeting, Moravian Church in America, Presbyterian Church in Canada, Presbyterian Church (U.S.A.), Reformed Church in America, United Church of Canada, United Church of Christ.

15. See Guin Ream Tuckett, *Living the Word* (St. Louis: Christian Board of Publications, 1977).

16. *Sharing the Light of Faith: National Catechetical Directory for Catholics of the United States* (Washington, D.C.: United States Catholic Conference, 1979). The process leading to the publication of this directory was a model of curriculum design, based on collaboration and consultation with thousands of Catholics throughout the country.

17. William Clayton Bower, *The Curriculum of Religious Education* (New York: Charles Scribner's Sons, 1925).

18. See chapter 2, above.

19. See especially John H. Westerhoff III, *Will Our Children Have Faith?* (New York: Seabury Press, 1976).

20. See John H. Westerhoff III, *Living the Faith Community* (Minneapolis: Winston Press, 1985); Gwen Kennedy Neville and John H. Westerhoff III, *Learning Through Liturgy* (New York: Seabury Press, 1978); and John H. Westerhoff III and William Willimon, *Liturgy and Learning Throughout the Life Cycle* (New York: Seabury Press, 1980).

21. C. Ellis Nelson, *Where Faith Begins* (Atlanta: John Knox Press, 1967). See esp. pp. 149–150, 183–185, 202–210.

22. Ibid., p. 202.

23. Gress and Purpel, *Curriculum,* p. 558.

24. Gabriel Moran, *Religious Education Development* (Minneapolis: Winston Press, 1983), pp. 160ff. See also Newmann and Oliver, "Education and Community," pp. 196ff.

25. William Walsh, *The Use of Imagination: Educational Thought and the Literary Mind* (New York: Barnes & Noble, 1960), pp. 55–56.

26. Maria Harris, *Teaching and Religious Imagination* (San Francisco: Harper & Row, 1987), p. 32.

27. Paulo Freire, *Pedagogy of the Oppressed* (New York: Herder & Herder, 1970), pp. 12–13, 20ff.

28. See Walter Burghardt, "What Is a Priest?" in *The Sacraments,* ed. Michael Taylor (New York: Alba House, 1981), pp. 157–170.

29. Elliot W. Eisner, *The Educational Imagination* (New York: Macmillan Co., 1979). See ch. 5, pp. 74–92.

Chapter 4. Koinonia: The Curriculum of Community

1. Gilbert Keith Chesterton, *Orthodoxy* (1943; Garden City, N.Y.: Doubleday & Co., Image Books, 1959), p. 85.

2. John H. Westerhoff III, *Will Our Children Have Faith?* (New York: Seabury Press, 1976).

3. Thomas Aquinas, *Summa Theologica,* trans. Fathers of the English Dominican Province (New York: Benziger Brothers, 1948), I, q. 39, a. 2, ad. 3.

4. Albert Camus, *The Rebel,* trans. Anthony Bower (New York: Alfred A. Knopf, 1954), p. 22.

5. See Rosemary Radford Ruether, *Sexism and God-Talk: Toward a Feminist Theology* (Boston: Beacon Press, 1984). See esp. ch. 8, "Ministry and Community for a People Liberated from Sexism."

6. Sheila Moriarty O'Fahey, "Pluralism and the Catholic Believer: Implications for Parish Planning," in *PACE 2* (Winona, Minn.: St. Mary's Press, 1971).

7. *Notre Dame Study of Catholic Parish Life.* "The Parish as Community," Report No. 10 (Notre Dame, Ind.: Institute for Pastoral and Social Ministry and the Center for the Study of Contemporary Society of the University of Notre Dame, March 1987), pp. 12–13.

8. The Notre Dame Study noted "frequency of conversations with pastor" third in importance for most people out of a possible fifteen choices, ranking only after "number of activities the person participates in" and "the sense that the parish met their social needs," to explore persons' attachment to the local parish. See p. 8.

9. William J. Bausch, *The Christian Parish* (Mystic, Conn.: Twenty-Third Publications, 1981), p. 218.

10. Notre Dame Study, p. 2.

11. See Kathleen McGinnis and James McGinnis, *Parenting for Peace and Justice* (Maryknoll, N.Y.: Orbis Books, 1981); Thomas Lickona, *Raising Good Children* (New York: Bantam Books, 1985); Annette Hollander, *How to Help Your Child Have a Spiritual Life* (New York: Bantam Books, 1982); and Gloria Durka and Joanmarie Smith, eds., *Family Ministry* (Minneapolis: Winston Press, 1980).

12. Gabriel Marcel, *Philosophy of Existence* (New York: Philosophical Library, 1949), pp. 25–26.

13. Gabriel Marcel, *Creative Fidelity* (New York: Farrar, Straus & Co., 1964), p. 28.

14. The tragedy and terror of family violence and the abuse of children are tragic and horrifying in part because they are characterized by the absence of these necessary elements as children grow up and as the adults in families are related to children and to one another.

15. Gabriel Moran, *No Ladder to the Sky* (San Francisco: Harper & Row, 1987), p. 67.

16. Walt Whitman, *Leaves of Grass,* ed. Emory Holloway (Garden City, N.Y.: Doubleday, Page & Co., 1926), pp. 305–306.

17. Moran, *No Ladder to the Sky,* pp. 74–75.

Chapter 5. Leiturgia: The Curriculum of Prayer

1. John H. Westerhoff III, *Living the Faith Community* (Minneapolis: Winston Press, 1985), p. 57. See also Gwen Kennedy Neville and John H. Westerhoff III, *Learning Through Liturgy* (New York: Seabury Press, 1978); and John H. Westerhoff III and William Willimon, *Liturgy and Learning Throughout the Life Cycle* (New York: Seabury Press, 1980).

2. See Michel Quoist, *Prayers* (New York: Sheed & Ward, 1963); Mark Link, *You* (Niles, Ill.: Argus Communications, 1976); and Anthony DeMello, *One Minute Wisdom* (New York: Doubleday & Co., Image Books, 1988).

3. See Linda Clark, Marian Ronan, and Eleanor Walker, *Image-Breaking/Image-Building: A Handbook for Creative Worship with Women of Christian Tradition* (New York: Pilgrim Press, 1981), esp. pp. 70–71; Janet Kalven and Mary I. Buckley, eds., *Women's Spirit Bonding* (New York: Pilgrim Press, 1984); and Rosemary Radford Ruether, *WomanGuides: Readings Toward a Feminist Theology* (Boston: Beacon Press, 1986).

4. Anthony deMello, *Sadhana: A Way to God* (St. Louis: Institute of Jesuit Sources, 1978), p. 3.

5. See Herbert Benson, *The Relaxation Response* (New York: Avon Books, 1975), pp. 162–163.

6. T. S. Eliot, *Four Quartets* (1943; New York: Harcourt Brace Jovanovich, 1968), p. 44.

7. Michael Warren, ed., *Readings and Resources in Youth Ministry* (Winona, Minn.: St. Mary's Press, 1987), p. 14.

8. For some resources, see Aileen A. Doyle, *Youth Retreats: Creating Sacred Space for Young People* (Winona, Minn.: St. Mary's Press, 1986); Charles Reutemann, *Let's Pray: Fifty Services for Praying Communities* (Winona, Minn.: St. Mary's Press, 1982); and idem, *Let's Pray 2* (Winona, Minn.: St. Mary's Press, 1983).

9. Westerhoff, *Living*, pp. 58–68.

10. Annie Dillard, *Teaching a Stone to Talk: Expeditions and Encounters* (San Francisco: Harper & Row, 1982), p. 40.

Chapter 6. Didache: The Curriculum of Teaching

1. Jacob Firet, *Dynamics in Pastoring* (Grand Rapids: Wm. B. Eerdmans Publishing Co., 1986), p. 58.

2. Ibid., p. 55.

3. See Paulo Freire, *Pedagogy of the Oppressed* (New York:

Herder & Herder 1970); idem, *Education for Critical Conscious-ness* (New York: Seabury Press, 1973); Thomas Green, *The Activities of Teaching* (New York: McGraw Hill Book Co., 1971); and Brian Wren, *Education for Justice* (Maryknoll, N.Y.: Orbis Books, 1977).

4. See *Christian Initiation Resources Reader,* vol. 1: Precate-chumenate; vol. 2: Catechumenate; vol. 3: Purification and En-lightenment; vol. 4: Mystagogia and Ministries (New York: William H. Sadlier, 1984).

5. James D. Smart, *The Rebirth of Ministry* (Philadelphia: Westminster Press, 1960), p. 66.

6. Karl Barth, *Church Dogmatics,* IV/3 (Edinburgh: T. & T. Clark, 1962), p. 867.

7. See Elisabeth Schüssler Fiorenza, *In Memory of Her: A Feminist Reconstruction of Christian Origins* (New York: Crossroad, 1983); and Phyllis Trible, *Texts of Terror* (Philadelphia: Fortress Press, 1984), for examples of this aspect of teaching.

8. Rainer Maria Rilke, *Letters to a Young Poet* (New York: W. W. Norton & Co., 1934), p. 33.

9. See Freire, *Pedagogy.*

10. See Maria Harris, *Teaching and Religious Imagination* (San Francisco: Harper & Row, 1987), p. xv.

11. Gabriel Moran, *No Ladder to the Sky* (San Francisco: Harper & Row, 1987), pp. 159–160ff.

12. See David Kolb, *Experiential Learning: Experience as the Source of Learning and Development* (Englewood Cliffs, N.J.: Prentice-Hall, 1983).

13. See Maria Harris, *Women and Teaching* (Mahwah, N.J.: Paulist Press, 1988); see also Mary Belenky, Blythe Clinchy, Nancy Goldberger, and Jill Tarule, *Women's Ways of Knowing* (New York: Basic Books, 1986).

14. Norma J. Everist, *Education Ministry in the Congregation: Eight Ways We Learn from One Another* (Minneapolis: Augsburg Publishing House, 1983).

15. Margot Stern Strom and William Parsons, *Facing History and Ourselves: Holocaust and Human Behavior* (Watertown, Mass.: Intentional Publications, 1982).

16. Thomas Groome, *Christian Religious Education: Sharing Our Story and Vision* (San Francisco: Harper & Row, 1980).

17. See the following Abingdon Press books by Donald L. Griggs: *Basic Skills for Church Teachers* (1985); *Planning for Teaching Church School* (1985); *Teaching Teachers to Teach*

(1974); *Translating the Good News Through Teaching Activities* (1980); and *Twenty New Ways of Teaching the Bible* (1979). See also Donald Griggs and Patricia Griggs, *Teaching and Celebrating Advent* (Nashville: Abingdon Press, 1980); and *Generations Learning Together* (Nashville: Abingdon Press, 1980).

18. Harris, *Teaching and Religious Imagination* pp. 46–59.

19. See Maria Harris, "Teaching: Forming and Transforming Grace," in C. Ellis Nelson, ed., *Congregations: Their Power to Form and Transform* (Atlanta: John Knox Press, 1988), pp. 238–263.

20. Jules Isaac, *The Teaching of Contempt* (New York: Holt, Rinehart & Winston, 1964).

Chapter 7. Kerygma: The Curriculum of Proclamation

1. C. F. Evans, "Kerygma," in *The Westminster Dictionary of Christian Theology,* ed. Alan Richardson and John Bowden (Philadelphia: Westminster Press, 1983), p. 316.

2. Eberhard Simons, "Kerygma," in *Sacramentum Mundi,* ed. Karl Rahner et al. (New York: Herder & Herder, 1969), p. 245.

3. Abraham Heschel, *The Prophets* (New York: Harper & Row, 1962), p. 5.

4. C. H. Dodd, "The 'Message' in the Gospels and Epistles," in *The Ministry of the Word,* ed. Paulins Milner (London: Burns & Oates, 1967), p. 45.

5. John McKenzie, "Kerygma," in *Dictionary of the Bible* (Milwaukee: Bruce Publishing Co., 1965), p. 638.

6. See Pierre-André Liege, "The Ministry of the Word: From Kerygma to Catechesis," in *Sourcebook for Modern Catechetics,* ed. Michael Warren (Winona, Minn.: St. Mary's Press, 1983), pp. 313–328.

7. John Donahue, "Biblical Perspectives on Justice," in *The Faith That Does Justice,* ed. John C. Haughey (New York: Paulist Press, 1977), pp. 69ff.

8. See Matthew Fox, *Compassion* (Minneapolis: Winston Press, 1979), p. vi.

9. Robert McAfee Brown, *Creative Dislocation* (Nashville: Abingdon Press, 1980), p. 129.

10. Walter Brueggemann, *The Prophetic Imagination* (Philadelphia: Fortress Press, 1978), p. 13.

11. Gustavo Gutiérrez, *A Theology of Liberation* (Maryknoll, N.Y.: Orbis Books, 1973), p. 308.

12. See Susanne Langer, *Feeling and Form* (New York: Charles Scribner's Sons, 1953).

13. Brown, *Creative Dislocation,* pp. 28–29.

14. Ignatius of Antioch, bishop and martyr, called the God out of whom the word came *Sige*—the Silence.

15. John Fry, *The Great Apostolic Blunder Machine* (New York: Harper & Row, 1978), pp. 174–175.

16. John Baptist Metz, "Facing the Jews: Christian Theology After Auschwitz," in *The Holocaust as Interruption,* ed. Elisabeth Schüssler Fiorenza and David Tracy, Concilium Volume 175 (Edinburgh: T. & T. Clark, 1984), pp. 26–33.

17. On advocacy, see Maria Harris, *Portrait of Youth Ministry* (Ramsey, N.J.: Paulist Press, 1981), pp. 142–172.

18. John Howard Yoder, *The Politics of Jesus* (Grand Rapids: Wm. B. Eerdmans Publishing Co., 1972).

19. Harry Fagan, *Empowerment: Skills for Parish Social Action* (New York: Paulist Press, 1979).

Chapter 8. Diakonia: The Curriculum of Service

1. Cited in Gabriel Moran, *No Ladder to the Sky* (San Francisco: Harper & Row, 1987), p. 67.

2. See Maria Harris, *Portrait of Youth Ministry* (Ramsey, N.J.: Paulist Press, 1981), "Diakonia: The Ministry of Troublemaking," pp. 23–26, 173–190.

3. Cited in Matthew Fox, *Original Blessing* (Santa Fe, N.M.: Bear & Co., 1983), p. 72.

4. Moran, *No Ladder,* p. 67.

5. Nel Noddings, *Caring: A Feminine Approach to Ethics and Moral Education* (Berkeley and Los Angeles: University of California Press, 1984). The theme of care is central in the philosophy of Martin Heidegger.

6. Carol Gilligan, *In a Different Voice: Psychological Theory and Women's Development* (Cambridge, Mass.: Harvard University Press, 1982).

7. E. Mansell Pattison, M.D., "Systems Pastoral Care," in *Journal of Pastoral Care,* vol. 26, no. 1 (March 1972), cited in Dieter Hessel, *Social Ministry* (Philadelphia: Westminster Press, 1982), p. 125.

8. See Franklin Littell, *The Crucifixion of the Jews* (New York: Harper & Row, 1975; Macon, Ga.: Mercer University Press, 1985), pp. 141–153, for an example of such a ceremony.

9. Hessel, *Social Ministry,* p. 151.

10. Ibid.

11. James B. Guinan, *Christianity and Crisis,* vol. 48, no. 8 (May 16, 1988), p. 191.

12. See Thomas F. O'Meara, *Theology of Ministry* (Ramsey, N.J.: Paulist Press, 1983), p. 200.

13. Ibid., pp. 136ff.

14. Hessel, *Social Ministry,* p. 77.

15. Abraham Heschel, *The Prophets* (New York: Harper & Row, 1962), p. xv.

Chapter 9. Facilitating the Fashioning

1. William Clayton Bower, *The Curriculum of Religious Education* (New York: Charles Scribner's Sons, 1925).

2. Ibid., pp. 207ff.

3. Among Herbart's works are *Allgemeine Pädagogik* (1806); *Umriss pädagogischer Vorlesungen* (1835); and *Outlines of Educational Doctrine* (New York, 1901).

4. Bower, *The Curriculum of Religious Education,* p. 208.

5. Ralph Tyler, *Basic Principles of Curriculum and Instruction* (Chicago: University of Chicago Press, 1950). For a perceptive commentary on the work of Tyler and the context surrounding it, see Elliot W. Eisner, *The Educational Imagination* (New York: Macmillan Co., 1979), pp. 8–24.

6. See Mary Boys, "Curriculum Thinking from a Roman Catholic Perspective," in *Religious Education,* vol. 75, no. 5 (September–October 1980), pp. 516–528.

7. Other approaches to designing curriculum are of course needed—political, sociological, psychological, ethical, and religious. However, I would still argue that fundamentally, to design something is to do artistic work. In addition, this approach has been slighted in the past in favor of the technical and mechanical. See Eisner, *The Educational Imagination,* pp. 109–126.

8. Eisner, *The Educational Imagination,* p. 128.

9. For this rendering of the term "steps," I am indebted to Judith Dorney. The notion of rhythm in education is a continuing, although minority, strand. See, e.g., John Dewey, *Art as Experience* (1934; New York: Capricorn, 1958), pp. 247ff., and Alfred North Whitehead, *The Aims of Education* (New York, 1929), pp. 15–28. The theme is developed at length in Maria

Harris, *Women and Teaching* (Mahwah, N.J.: Paulist Press, 1988), pp. 13–16.

10. See Maria Harris, *Teaching and Religious Imagination* (San Francisco: Harper & Row, 1987), pp. 26–40.

11. For an extensive and complementary description of this first step of fashioning, named by the authors as Leader Development/Support, see Shirley Heckman and Iris Ferren, *Creating the Congregation's Educational Ministry* (Elgin, Ill.: Brethren Press, 1976), pp. 53–62.

12. Eisner, *The Educational Imagination,* pp. 253–338, offers examples of how this kind of reflection on process is done.

13. Examples of an explicit curriculum in conflict with an implicit curriculum might be in a church that proclaims concerns for poverty but tithes nothing of its own budget for the poor; claims a love and concern for children but tolerates abuse of children in its midst; calls itself a community open to all but supports the closing of integrated schools. The implicit curriculum is also revelatory when one examines curriculum in terms of guiding images and metaphors and in terms of who makes decisions regarding curriculum and curriculum implementation.

14. Examples of the null curriculum might be the absence of wheelchair access for those who need it or signing for the deaf or aid to families with Downs syndrome children. The null curriculum may also become apparent at this step if a church realizes it has no service programs or no support for prayer outside the Sunday worship. For a helpful publication in this area, see the Council on Interracial Books for Children *Bulletin* (1841 Broadway, New York, N.Y. 10023) which promotes antiracist, antisexist, and antistereotypical education in an eight-times-a-year publication.

15. To assist people to contemplate the curriculum of education in their own situations, I often suggest the following exercise: For our next meeting, assess the overall curriculum of education in the place where you live and work in terms of *(a)* the three curricula: explicit, implicit, and null; *(b)* goals, visions, and stated purposes; *(c)* assumptions about teaching; *(d)* unresolved issues or those in the process of being resolved; and *(e)* guiding imagery of education.

16. See *Cooperative Curriculum Project: The Church's Educational Ministry: A Curriculum Plan* (St. Louis: Bethany Press, 1965).

17. See Exercise 3, below, "Holding On and Letting Go."

18. These are not meant as rhetorical questions or designed simply for discussion. They are questions intended as tools, chisels for change.

19. For assistance in conflict resolution, see Thomas Sweetser and Carol Wisniewski Holden, *Leadership in a Successful Parish* (San Francisco: Harper & Row, 1987), pp. 94–107.

20. The *Kerygma* Program, 300 Mt. Lebanon Boulevard, Suite 205, Pittsburgh, Pa. 15234.

21. See James B. Dunning, *New Wine: New Wineskins. The Rite of Christian Initiation of Adults* (New York: William H. Sadlier, 1981).

22. National Office of Renew, Kearny, N.J., *Renew: An Overview* (Ramsey, N.J.: Paulist Press, 1984).

23. For description of such churches, see Maria Harris, *Portrait of Youth Ministry* (Ramsey, N.J.: Paulist Press, 1981), pp. 176–181.

24. Facing History and Ourselves Foundation, 25 Kennard Road, Brookline, Mass. 02146.

25. Thomas Fenton, ed., *Education for Justice* (Maryknoll, N.Y.: Orbis Books, 1975).

26. Among the resources that describe and present alternative forms for curriculum including art, sport, and other physical involvement are Doug Adams and Diane Apostolos-Cappadona, eds., *Art as Religious Studies* (New York: Crossroad, 1987); Ingrid Rogers, *Swords Into Plowshares: A Collection of Plays About Peace and Social Justice* (Elgin, Ill.: Brethren Press, 1983); Gloria Durka and Joanmarie Smith, eds., *Aesthetic Dimensions of Religious Education* (New York: Paulist Press, 1979); "Religious Education Through Fantasy," a special issue of *British Journal of Religious Education*, vol. 10, no. 1 (Autumn 1987); and Gertrud Mueller Nelson, *To Dance with God: Family Ritual and Community Celebration* (Mahwah, N.J.: Paulist Press, 1986).

Index